Jane Newton was born in England but brought up in Africa. She is a trained counsellor and worked for fifteen years as a surgery counsellor for three NHS practices. All her clients were sent by the doctors or other medical professionals. Both her personal life and her experience in counselling have given her deep insights into human nature. She now lives in the south west of England.

KNOW YOURSELF,
UNDERSTAND OTHERS

Jane Newton

KNOW YOURSELF,
UNDERSTAND OTHERS

Vanguard Press

VANGUARD PAPERBACK

© Copyright 2019
Jane Newton

A CIP catalogue record for this title is
available from the British Library.

ISBN 978 1 78465 556 3

*Vanguard Press is an imprint of
Pegasus Elliot MacKenzie Publishers Ltd.*
www.pegasuspublishers.com

First Published in 2019

**Vanguard Press
Sheraton House Castle Park
Cambridge England**

Printed & Bound in Great Britain

Dedication

To Mike

Introduction

This book does exactly what it says in the title. It challenges opinions, and queries your understanding about many life situations. No one can honestly say they know themselves or anyone else. We are continually facing new situations, forming ideas and attitudes. Life presents a lot of ups and downs, and we try and cope somehow. Anxiety and depression are on the increase in society. Is this because of the way we look at life or is life getting more difficult? A small change can transform a life. This book is jargon free. It opens up ways of thinking, giving clearer understanding of others, and new directions in life.

Upbringing, sex, mental illness and bereavement are some of the subjects explored. There are exercises and ideas, helpful for individuals in their own lives, and for those training to support or understand others.

Imagine everyone is a rose bush. Maybe you are too young to have bloomed yet, or any blooms you may have had have faded. Lack of care, damage, or even being in the shade can cause difficulties. All rose bushes need nurturing, understanding and possibly pruning, to bloom again. Are you like a climbing rose, needing to be propped up until you gain more confidence? Maybe you are like a miniature rose battling to be seen through the weeds. Clearing the ground around you will help. There may be damage from neglect or an accident, requiring extra loving care. Whichever type of rose you may identify with, you will have thorns. Do you recognise your own faults and accept failure in others? Have you hurt someone or even yourself? This book will encourage you to look at who you are and consider the emotions you, and others, may experience at different times of life.

Life may be a bed of roses after all!

CONTENTS

EXERCISES

CHAPTER ONE – YOUR CHILDHOOD CONFRONTED

Are you lucky to have had a loving family and a wonderful upbringing? Looking back, do you remember sunny days and a happy childhood? For many, life was not like that at all. Perhaps there were illnesses, or a death, or a difficult past relationship? Was there verbal, physical or sexual abuse? Bullying at school or sibling rivalry may have made your life hard. Poverty could have been a problem, or the insecurity of not having a permanent home. There are so many ways your childhood could have been spoilt.

Most parents do not have any training as to how to bring up children. They do their best and hope things turn out well. Unfortunately, some parents fail to understand what is needed, perhaps not giving love or understanding. In some cases, circumstances prevent them from being ideal role models. Your parents' divorce or separation may have affected you badly. Was there some violence or rowing? Maybe you never knew your parents. Relatives or foster parents may have brought you up, or care workers in a children's home. Were you adopted?

Everything in your background has an impact on how you see life and can affect self-esteem and confidence. You may not remember much at all about your childhood. Some people, consciously or unconsciously, block out difficult times. Alternatively, it could just be a lack of memory. Are there areas in your life you have never been able to share with anyone? Have you ever tried to express your feelings? Perhaps you were ignored or your opinions rejected. Flashbacks may spoil your life now. Each person has a lifetime of experiences that have formed their character and attitudes. The way you react, your moods, your outlook and your expectations, all form your personality. You will never understand yourself completely. Each situation encountered in life sparks off new feelings and emotions, but understanding why they happen may help.

PARENTING

How you were treated as a very young child can influence how you feel about yourself for the rest of your life. Imagine the situation you were born into. Were your parents very young? Perhaps they were not married and the pregnancy upset the family. Alternatively, were your parents forced into marriage they may not have wanted? Were you a planned baby or a surprise? Was there a problem conceiving or a difficult pregnancy? Postnatal depression might have followed. With lots of other children to look after, an elderly parent or a demanding job, the time spent with you may have been limited. If your parents were not getting on well, were there continual rows, accusations and threats. What attention did you get? Picture yourself as a child and how you would do things differently if you were in a parental role.

If you did not receive all the emotional attention and support you wanted as a child, you may have picked up the idea that no one cares and that you have to cope with life alone. You may have started a pattern of holding on to problems. Thinking no one is interested, you presume it is because you are not lovable. A lifelong pattern of feeling worthless can result. Your reaction might have been to be naughty. Any attention is better than none. Alternatively, you may have become withdrawn and shunned relationships. Did you rebel as a teenager? Do you feel you have to be different to get noticed, or blend in with those around you, hiding behind others?

A break-up in your parents' relationship can influence how you feel about yourself. Maybe you have never known your father or mother. Perhaps you feel, quite wrongly, that if you had been good they would have stayed together. One parent may be hated because of the effect the break-up has had on the other. There can be a lot of anger that one parent has never got in touch or has let you down. It helps to remember that once your mum and dad did like each other and, in most cases, were two consenting adults. Break-up was probably never intended. There are always two sides to every story and the blame is usually fifty-fifty whatever one parent says. Sadly, some children can be the result of a rape, a difficult concept to live with.

The bitterness, recriminations and accusations after any break-up can be really upsetting. Some children are used as a weapon or blamed for the problem. Were you asked to choose who you lived with? Terrible guilt feelings can follow. Maybe one parent confided in you, involving you in adult problems and emotions long before you were an adult yourself. You may have been influenced enough to hate one parent, not really understanding why.

If a parent never got in touch, it is possible they do not care, but often it is for different reasons. Seeing their ex- partner or you may have broken their heart. They were no longer allowed to get close. The rejection and worthlessness they may have felt would have been made easier if they stayed away. The jealousy of a new partner could have made contact difficult. Perhaps one partner never allowed the other one near, blaming them rather than admitting the rejection. Do not jump to the conclusion that you are not loved. Getting in touch with an estranged parent can be difficult, but for some it allays fears and often changes any preconceived ideas. Unfortunately, witnessing arguments, violence and hatred does not help your understanding of how relationships work. Your parents were supposed to be your role models, and yet you may not like what you see nor have any idea how a good relationship works.

Parents who suffer from illness or depression can unwittingly put great pressure on a child. Did you have to take on a caring role? This would have made you grow up fast and take on responsibilities long before most other children. You may have had to do chores instead of going out to play. Did anyone share your burden? What did you do if you felt guilty or resentful? The death of a parent is always tragic. It may have caused you to miss out on childhood, as you were robbed of security and innocence. Did you feel you needed to fill the gap in the home, taking on the parental role looking after younger children or caring for those who had been bereaved. Were you allowed to go to the funeral? Perhaps no one listened to your grief. The death of a brother, sister, or other family member may have long-term implications too. The chapter on bereavement may help your understanding.

Was there a favourite in your family? Jealousies and resentment can be the result, and confidence diminished. Comparison with a cleverer brother or sister can cause animosity between siblings. What about grandparents? Did they have an influential role on your life? Often grandparents give the love parents are unable to offer. There may have been a neighbour, aunt or family friend who had a significant impact on your childhood, giving you a feeling of self-worth.

DISCIPLINE

Most family homes are a battlefield at times. Fair discipline, given with understanding, is important to give guidelines. It is often for safety reasons too. Did you suffer from harsh or unfair treatment? Were you shut in a lot, degraded or totally ignored as a punishment? Parents do not always agree on how children should be treated. One parent may be kind while the other is an ogre, possibly compensating for the leniency. Their own background and experience may be repeated, however harsh. It did them no harm, they might say. Were you verbally or physically abused? Your parents may have been very strict regarding your social life, where you went, or the company you kept. Did you have disagreements about your religious beliefs, racial attitudes or views regarding sex? Sometimes a parent becomes very jealous of a child. Their own feelings of inadequacy or vulnerability may cause them to put you down or make you suffer in some way. Would you do things differently if you were a parent? What sort of guidelines would you give?

SEX ABUSE

Were you sexually abused as a child or experienced rape? So many emotions flow from this sort of experience. You may have been struggling with your feelings for years. Do others in the family know what happened or is it your secret? It is important to emphasise, whatever happened, it was not your fault, although the feelings of guilt can sometimes be overwhelming. No one asks to be raped or abused. It is a terrible crime. In any abuse you are not responsible. No one should subject a child to sexual interference of any sort. If it has happened to you, talking about it or getting help can enable you to move on in your life.

Child abuse may have been perpetrated by a father, step- parent, mother's friend, grandfather, babysitter, brother, uncle, neighbour, teacher or friend. In some cases, it might be by your mother or another woman. Was the abuse homosexual? The abuse may have been by someone you loved or trusted. Whoever the person or persons were, they robbed you of your choice of when and how to explore your own sexuality and experience sex. It should have been your choice in your time.

Being introduced into an adult sexual world when only a child can cause a lot of anguish and misunderstandings. Was there violence, aggression or threats? Possibly you were lulled into a sexual union by false love, presents or money. The modern method of computer grooming is a growing crime. It may have been your own need for attention that was exploited. As a child, you may not have thought it wrong, thinking all other children experience the same thing. The sexual feelings might have been enjoyable which will add to your confusion. Conversely, it might have been horrible, violent, painful or frightening. Your memories may be vivid and upsetting, or alternatively you may only have a dim recollection of what happened. A smell, a touch, a sound or sexual contact may bring it all back.

Telling someone of the abuse can be difficult. What if you were blamed, no one believed you or it ruined your parents' or someone else's relationship? You may be concerned that you will be ostracised by friends, rejected from a group or lose the love of someone. The reaction of those you tell may be to ask you to forget, make you feel bad or, in some cases, reject you from the home. You may feel dirty, wondering if you give out some sign and hate yourself. The abuse might have been a one-off occasion or continual. The fact that you did not stop it is not your fault. You may look back now as an adult and wonder why you put up with things, but don't forget you were a child. To emphasise again, it is never your fault. Child sexual abuse is a crime and the adult perpetrators should be punished. If you feel you would like to take some action, it is never too late.

Talk about it, share your concerns and get help. You may prevent others having to suffer abuse too.

Sometimes sexual experience in childhood can be from other children of a similar age. Trying to understand the opposite sex or having an interest in how your own body works is natural, but for some experimentation can go too far. Being found out can have difficult consequences and is not always handled sensitively. Again, remember you were only a child and you would not have understood the implications. Get help if you need to. You will be believed. The chapter on sex might help your sexual understanding.

SCHOOLING

Do you remember your school days affectionately? They may have been the best or worst days of your life. Teachers can have a huge effect, in positive and negative ways. A bad teacher can make you feel an outcast and worthless, while another teacher can open up new exciting avenues to explore. Sometimes a learning difficulty is overlooked, making you feel useless, while struggling to keep up. There may have been other problems at school. Bullying is not always understood or dealt with appropriately. Were you a victim? Children can be so cruel. They often pick on anyone different or vulnerable. Perhaps you suffered from racial abuse, ridicule about where you lived or the clothes you wore. It is a method used by other pupils to assert domination, often because of their own inadequacies. There can be long-term implications, resulting in education being disrupted or abandoned altogether. Maybe you were the one doing the bullying.

Were you sent away to school? The home circumstances at the time may influence how you feel about your experience. Home sickness or loneliness can be difficult for a child. You may have been sent to a privileged school where academic pressure caused stress, or just sent away to get you out of an environment. Having to make new friends is not always easy. Schooling can be the most wonderful time of your life, but for some it is a nightmare.

SELF-WORTH

Your childhood can have a big influence on how you see yourself. Liking who you are is important in making good relationships. This does not mean you being boastful and conceited, but just appreciating you have worth. To cover inner pain, you may have always cracked jokes or try to be the life and soul of a party. The insecurity is still there. You may have put on a lot of weight and eat for comfort. Alternatively, you may always be worried about weight or looks, thinking perfection in appearance is a way to solve inner problems or make friends. Some turn to drugs or alcohol to try and get rid of the feelings, only making matters worse. Do you self-harm in an attempt to punish yourself or relieve tensions? Perhaps you have a cleaning phobia, trying to clean away memories. Recognise that you were not born bad. It is only through circumstances that you feel unlovable.

Leaving home and coping with life on your own may not be as you imagined. Money problems, responsibilities and work pressures can be overwhelming at first. Coping with loneliness, a new environment, making new friends and missing home can all be very stressful. Talk to others about how they cope, and get help. With new understandings you can become much more positive about yourself.

Have you had a romantic relationship that has gone wrong? The fairy tales have a lot to answer for. Not many first loves will end happily ever after. Resulting bitterness or resentment can affect a new partnership. You may hang back from commitment, in an attempt not to be hurt again. One or both of you may not have been ready for a commitment. Recognise and accept the part you played in starting the relationship, and understand the role you may have played in any break-up. This can prevent a similar problem occurring. The chapter on surviving relationships might help. Perhaps you are gay. It is not always easy to admit to the feelings. Parents do not necessarily understand, and some people's prejudices can be very hurtful. Talk to someone and get support.

A difficult past life or childhood need not be negative. Experience of rejection, pain, grief, disappointment or guilt can help you know more about life. Imagine how boring you would be if nothing had ever happened in your life. The knowledge, courage and insights gained have given you wisdom and valued understanding. People recognising your experience might already ask for your advice. With your experience of life, you may be able to help a partner, children or others to overcome their problems in the future.

Exercise (i) Getting to know yourself.

Here is an exercise to make you think about who you really are. You may find it difficult to reveal your true self to others, hiding behind the persona you choose to project. What would people think if they knew the real you? What are your positive points and what are your negatives? Put them down in columns as illustrated. Be honest with yourself. There are three examples of other people's personalities. A list of possible characteristics follows to give you some ideas. This is an interesting exercise to do about someone else too. If you are in a relationship, why not write one for each other. Compare notes and see if you really understand each other's personality.

Example (1): (twenty-six-year-old woman)

POSITIVE   NEGATIVE

Caring   Hopeless
with money
Understanding   Moody
Friendly   Untidy
Good cook   Jealous
Average looks
Artistic

Example (2): (thirty-year-old man)

Hard worker   Bad temper
Good with money   Sulks
Good sense of humour
Sporty
Likes animals
Happy

Example (3): (fifty-two-year-old man)

Amusing   Grumpy
Generous   Drinker
Honest   Lazy
Clean and tidy

Ideas for your own character assessment

intelligent	TV addict
friendly	possessive
clean and tidy	jealous
creative	overweight
good with money	extravagant
animal lover	drinker
good-looking	nag
gentle	short-tempered
religious	vain
tolerant	takes drugs
good cook	insecure
generous	computer addict
thoughtful	lazy
mature	irresponsible
musical	demanding
kind	doesn't listen
artistic	fussy
sense of humour	swears
fit	irritable
good sexually	cannot relate
affectionate	judgemental
fun	secretive
sense of humour	hoarder
practical	clumsy
social	angry
domesticated	moody
likes children	smoker

hard worker	critical
enjoys reading	untidy
communicates well	snores
outdoor person	

CHAPTER TWO – THE TROUBLED INNER YOU

No one really knows what goes on inside you. You probably do not understand yourself at times. Most of us are such a mixture of emotions, having good and bad days. Do you have down days for no apparent reason? Perhaps there are feelings that no one loves you or cares. Worrying about what others think could be dominating your life, making socialising a problem. Will you have the confidence to talk to people, what should you wear? What if no one talks to you? Despite going out, you can feel very lonely in a crowd.

It could be work getting you down. Are you frightened to ask for a rise or to speak to your boss? Colleagues may be difficult or perhaps you are not feeling valued or fulfilled. Your own relationship could be in trouble. Are there sexual difficulties or some misunderstandings? There are so many disappointments, losses, pressures, stresses and expectations in life. Covering up your emotions despite what you feel inside is not always easy. If you told others of how you really feel, what do you think they would say? Do you imagine others all manage their lives well? Feelings of inadequacy are common. Not being able to cope is not a sign of weakness or failure.

Worry may be your constant companion. Do you worry about things of the past or things of the future? So often we worry about what we have said or done. Others may have forgotten the incident or forgiven ages ago, but the anxiety is still there. Your health may be a concern. Do you think the worst if you have a pain, imagining a terrible illness or even death? When memory fails, do you worry that senility is setting in? It is important to look after yourself and seek help when necessary but worry can take over your life.

Problems caused by family or friends can pull you down. Do you take on all their worries as well? If a loved one is late home, do you imagine there has been an accident, an affair or some disaster? Thinking of these possibilities may cause you to get emotional, feel inadequate or vulnerable. It is nature's way of an emotional practice run. Having a good cry helps. We all have to face losses or problems in our lives, but some worries can be unfounded. Once faced with a real problem, you may not react in the way you imagined at all. Alternatively, having imagined the consequences, you may have worked out a system of coping already. There is a lot of truth in the saying, 'a problem shared is a problem halved'. If you talk to others about your feelings, you will probably find many feel the way you do. Are you one of those people who worry if they do not have a worry? Be comforted in the fact that you are possibly a good strategic planner.

ANXIETY AND DEPRESSION

Feeling totally out of control emotionally is very disturbing. These inner feelings can be sparked off by nothing much at all. Alternatively, you may be trying to come to terms with a major disappointment or a death of someone who means a lot to you. Perhaps there is a broken close relationship, a life- threatening illness or a bad experience. Financial problems or a job loss may be the cause. Bad times can affect anyone and totally dominate your life and those around you. You are not going mad, although it does feel like it.

Concentration may be the first thing that goes. You forget things or put things in the wrong place. Sleeping can become difficult. You may not want to eat. Mood swings are common, often with aggression or temper. Perhaps you cannot stop crying. There may be palpitations, headaches or you break out in spots. Any activity may feel like a chore as you struggle with tiredness. If you are in a relationship, affection shown might be rejected, making sex a problem. Have you lost your sex drive completely? Emptiness and helplessness may cripple your everyday life, making living seem worthless. You may feel like running away.

Hard as it is to believe, but in most cases the feelings are not permanent. You are almost bound to fail in life sometimes, but that does not mean you are a total failure. If you are not able to cope at all with your daily tasks, or the feelings of hopelessness go on for two weeks or more, go and see your doctor. Grief is a natural response to a loss, but deep depression is an illness and can be treated. The chapter on mental illness will give you more insight.

PANIC ATTACKS

Panic attacks are quite common. You will not die of a panic attack, but it may feel like you will. There are different ways people are affected. Fear may suddenly take hold, or you may react to an irrational sense of danger. You may feel your heart racing, not being able to breathe properly and your thoughts all jumbled. Perhaps you feel dizzy, sweat, feel you are choking or shake uncontrollably. Some people think they are having a heart attack. Discuss your symptoms with your doctor. To help at the time of the attack, try to breathe slowly or blow out air. Find a wall to lean against or sit down. An attack can be quite short or last up to fifteen minutes or more. The fear of having another attack can feed into your anxieties.

POSSIBLE REASONS FOR ANXIETY OR DEPRESSION

Feeling down is often an accumulation of losses. The losses or failures can include many things. The list below may help you to analyse the losses that have happened to you.

Job loss
Relationship

Parents split up
Failed exams

Lost sight or hearing
An affair
Assaulted
Never loved

Teenagehood difficulties
Miscarriage
Accused wrongly
Unemployed

Failed career ambitions
Witness to shocking event

Death of a family member or friend
Unable to have a child
Abused
Never had the childhood you wanted
Bad parenting
Money problems
Loss of limb, mobility or fitness
Face or body changed or scarred
Falling out with parents/relatives
Raped
House burgled or burnt
Death of a much loved pet
Sexual humiliation
Homesickness

34

A move away from home/area	Drugs or alcohol
	Bullied at school
Car Accident	
Child born disabled/ill	Redundancy
Problems in relationship	Abortion
In care	Illness
Fallen out with best friend	Violence
Broken relationship	Enforced retirement
In prison	Unwanted pregnancy
Work stress	
Illness	

There are many other problems. No doubt you can think of some relative to you.

The following illustration may help to understand how and why you feel like you do. Imagine a box inside you called your stress box. Over the years you put in all your losses and disappointments. After each loss you close the lid and carry on. One day the lid will not close. The box is full. When you try to put in the next disappointment or stress, out pours all the past emotion and you cannot gain control. No amount of trying can get the lid down. It can make you very tired while you try to get control. Unfortunately, some turn to drink or drugs, trying to stop the feelings of helplessness as emotion pours out. The emotion returns when the effect of the drug or alcohol wears off. More drinks or drugs make matters worse. This is when addiction can start. Be warned. It will just add to your problem.

Here are examples of what caused crises in the lives of two individuals.

The straight lines in the boxes signify good times. The crosses depict stress or problems.

Example (1): Woman aged twenty-one

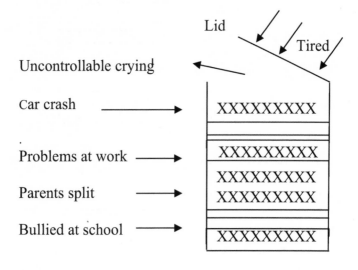

Example (2): Man aged eighteen

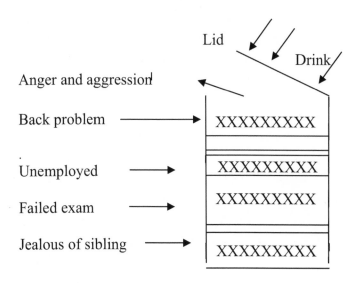

Consider all the losses and problems that may be relevant to you. Draw your own box.

Friends or a partner might find your emotions difficult to understand if you do not explain. If people have no experience of things going wrong in their life (yet), they may tell you to pull yourself together or snap out of it. How often have you heard people suggest a night out or a treat of some sort will sort you out? There is no quick fix. Cry as much as you can. A lot of men find this difficult as they have programmed themselves not to show emotion. A sad record or film will help. Allow yourself to cry or grieve for past losses and disappointments.

If you are usually the one who cares for others, it can be a difficult and lonely time, needing care for yourself for a change. You will not have the energy or inclination to help others, yet people may still expect you to be there for them. The reason is, you are a carer surrounded by takers. There is nothing wrong with being a taker, as they are needy. Under normal circumstances, it may make you feel good that you are there for them and can help. Unfortunately, takers do not suddenly become carers. Find others who will understand.

Friends may be wonderful and help a lot when things go wrong in your life, but you may find some let you down. They may be caught up with their own problems and, although sympathetic, may not want to get involved, or feel inadequate. Do not condemn people too quickly if they are not there for you. There are caring people out there who will help you. Do not be afraid to ask. Remember what it feels like when someone asks you to help. Did you feel needed and flattered? Give them a chance to use their caring side too and help you for a change, if they can.

Getting better and feeling back on track takes time, often a lot longer than imagined. You need the space to express emotion. Do not fight the feelings. Allow yourself to fall apart. As things get easier, try and get more active. Self-pity and isolation do not help. Blaming others or carrying bitterness will not help either. Seek to change yourself. Dress properly, eat well and keep clean. Keep up your standards where possible. Give yourself little treats. In time, your sense of well-being and self-esteem will improve, but do not expect too much too quickly. The problem will go away or you will learn to live with it. It is not a battle and you are not expected to fight.

Here are two ways to look at the problem. It is like being under a large black cloud. The cloud goes right round you and down to the floor. You can try to hit it, punch it, run away from it, go on holiday, get angry or jump up and down. The cloud just stays with you. The best thing to do is to sit down in the middle and cry. There is no use struggling. The cloud will lift when it is ready to go and not before. No amount of energy expended will make it disappear sooner. Another way of understanding your situation is to imagine you are sitting in a muddy pit. It has very steep sides. There is no way out. You trudge around in the mud. Each day, you wake up wondering how you are going to get through the next twenty-four hours. Everything seems pointless. One day there is a ladder. You may not see it at first or ignore it. There is a way out and you will be free.

To build an inner strength, imagine you have a solid rod down the middle of you. It is strong and will not bend. This rod is the inner you, the person, the soul if you like. It belongs to you and stays with you always. No one can take it away, bend it or break it. Relationships may flounder, accidents may happen or illness may take its toll, but nothing happens to your rod. It might wobble a bit occasionally, but like a wobbly man, it comes back. During really bad times, it is something to cling on to. Even if you are ill in bed, your inner rod is still there, the real you, your indestructible centre.

Some people turn to faith during a difficult time. What about your spiritual growth? Getting to know about a religion can give you a sense of purpose in life. Knowing God loves you, whatever happens, is a great reassurance for some. A faith does not mean you will avoid problems, but you may feel supported through any suffering. Becoming involved in a community could bring new friends. Joining an evening class or club might broaden your horizons. A new interest, the occasional treat or a holiday to look forward to, can help.

Having coped with a bad period in your life can bring a better understanding of society. The insights gained may give you a new life skill and the opportunity to help others' suffering too. You may be more tolerant in work or in the family, recognising others difficulties.

Exercise (ii) Relaxation
Try and relax. Sit on a chair with your feet flat on the floor. Rest your arms on your legs with the palms of

your hands facing upwards. Think about each part of your body in turn, starting with your toes and working upwards. Tell them to relax. Feet relax, knees relax, hips relax, bottom muscles relax and back relax. Tell your arms to relax, your neck, your arms, your shoulders and your hands...Relax. Drop your head. Let your tongue relax. Close your eyes. Feel the tingling sensation in your fingers as if all the stress is passing down your arms to the tips of your fingers and out into the air. Hear your breathing. Try and keep the position for a while, checking things are relaxed. You can do this exercise lying down as well. It may help you to get to sleep.

If you are facing a stressful situation or are troubled in any way, you may unconsciously tense round your shoulders. Just stop for a moment and relax. Drop your shoulders down as far as they can go. If you can, close your eyes and slowly count to ten. Slow down your breathing as you count. Being aware of your tension, you are halfway to eliminating it.

CHAPTER THREE — YOUR SEXUAL SECRETS REVEALED

When were you first sexually aware? For many children it is the discovery of masturbation, often a secret pleasure taken into adulthood. For others it will be noticing the body changes. Hair sprouts in different places. Girls become curvier and boys' voices start sounding croaky. Boys may be conscious of their balls dropping and starting to have wet dreams, while girls get breasts and periods begin. The actual age of change may differ considerably. Feelings and emotions can be muddling at this time, and teenage behaviour is renowned for mercurial outbursts.

Did your parents explain the facts of life or were you left to find out through friends, other family members or school? Despite all the talk about sex education, there is a lot of ignorance and confusion. Some find sex a very difficult subject to discuss.

Periods can be very different for each girl. Maybe you have never had problems, but some suffer with heavy periods, stomach ache or back ache. Each month the menstrual cycle can be a reassurance of female maturity or can be a burden, restricting normal activity. For some it is a sign of lost youth and freedom seen as a bind to be endured for years. Gym, swimming or sport may be difficult and cause embarrassment if no one understands why you are unable to take part.

Do you have sexual feelings you do not understand? Are you homosexual, bisexual or feel you are in the wrong body. It may be isolating or worrying as you struggle with the expectation of what others may consider normal or acceptable. Talking to someone who understands may give reassurance and support, as there are plenty of people who feel similar. The internet may be of some help too. Allowing yourself to be true to your feelings can be a considerable relief.

How long do you remain a virgin? You may want to save yourself until marriage, or for when you feel ready. Sex under sixteen is illegal. Just say NO if you do not want sex. Most partners accept rejection with understanding. An abusive, challenging or aggressive response is very upsetting. You have a right to decide for yourself. For most people, the first sexual encounter is fun and loving. Each is seeking to please the other. Unfortunately, for some the experience is sordid, secretive, unpleasant and painful. A partner may just be seeking self-gratification, and feelings or emotions are not relevant. Being accused of being frigid, inadequate or a failure can be very hurtful and ruin sexual confidence.

What was your first experience like? You may have been left thinking 'What is all the fuss about?' Alternatively, it may be the start of a desire to have as much sex as possible. The sex drive can be very strong, dominating your thoughts and actions. Maybe you did not like it and were put off sex for a while? Did you go out of your way to lose your virginity? For some it is something to get over with, while others see it as a rite of passage into an adult world, thinking it makes them more sophisticated. Were you flattered by attention, not wanting to be rejected and anxious to please? Maybe you were in love. Perhaps your first experience was as a newly married partner.

Whether it is a fumbling experimentation while you and your partner are inexperienced, or with a partner who seems to know about life, unfortunately pregnancy can be the unintended outcome. To say no, or stop and talk about contraception might seem churlish and unromantic at the time. Contraception advice given by parents or school is not always put into practice. There are plenty of opportunities to find out about contraception. It is the responsibility of both sexes.

Sex is certainly not always used in a loving relationship. It may be used to punish the opposite sex or to try and prove virility or attractiveness. Perhaps a past experience is the reason for promiscuity, or peer pressure leads to casual sex. Commitment for some is certainly not intended. Getting pregnant or catching a disease may be by accident, but is often caused by lack of judgment rather than lack of knowledge. Having a lot of sex with different partners does not mean you are necessarily any good at sex. The chances of something going wrong are increased and your self- esteem is rarely enhanced.

Grooming by older men is a very serious matter. Flattery, presents or promises are used to lure unsuspecting girls and boys into sexual activity. Once involved, threats, violence or possibly blackmail is used to perpetuate sexual activity and prostitution. Similarly, sexual predators use the internet to lull girls or boys into a sexual relationship. Sending sexual photos online or meeting up with complete strangers unaccompanied can be very dangerous. Inexperience, looking for love, seeking sex, or just wanting excitement can lead to a lifetime of regret or shame if you realise how you were used.

If you experience rape, report it. Having your right to your own body forcibly taken from you is devastating. Soft talking, kind words, threats or apologies do not make up for the fact you have been raped. Do not carry the emotional burden of the experience. There is help, and whatever the circumstances of the event, it is not your fault.

Sexual understanding is an extremely important part of a partnership and a source of great enjoyment when things are going well. Discussing each other's likes and dislikes and experimenting can all add to the experience. Alternatively, sex can be an area of great unhappiness. Problems can arise when two people have very different sexual appetites or attitudes. Whether sex, fucking, bonking, making love, or whatever you may like to call it, is many times a day, a few times a week, once a year or never, it is entirely up to you, as long as you both agree. If sex is good, sexual adventure can be enjoyed into old age. Sex can be loving, funny, romantic, comforting, exciting, fun or tender. In contrast it can be boring, a chore, painful, unfulfilling, violent or threatening.

In most relationships sex is frequent at the start. Partners are usually anxious to please. Over time, sexual desire can change, and this can cause a lot of misunderstanding. You may start to feel unloved, neglected and hurt unless there is communication. Mood, tiredness, weight loss or gain, body image, stress, cleanliness, smell, the venue, shyness, pain or medication can cause problems. The same approach from a partner can get a totally different response on different days. For some women, it can make a big difference as to how sexy she feels depending on the time of the month. Sometimes, if there has been any sexual abuse in the past, there may be flashbacks making relaxation difficult. After pregnancy a woman may not want sex as she adjusts to the new life and gets over the birth. Perhaps sexual feelings have diminished because muscle tone or weight has changed during pregnancy. Similarly, a partner may not feel so sexy after an operation or change in body image, or the menopause. In some cases, medical help might be needed. A sad or emotional loss or shock, redundancy, illness or life crisis can cause partners to go off sex. Fear of pregnancy or a sheltered upbringing may influence your attitude too.

Premature ejaculation can cause a lot of disappointment and misunderstanding. Similarly, problems in getting an erection can cause difficulties. Do you explain your problem or expect your partner to accept the situation? If you do not want sex, do you manage to say no with understanding or is there a row? Perhaps you are rejected and immediately feel you are no longer loved or wanted. If you are turned down a lot, there may be an underlying problem. Discuss your feelings and do not immediately assume there is an affair. Men often find it difficult to ask for help as they consider their manhood threatened. In a lot of partnerships, one partner has a higher sex drive. Couples have to work out a compromise. It is worth dealing with any difficulties and getting help where necessary so you are both able to enjoy a full life together.

Relaxation and enjoyment of sex is very difficult for some. You may be scared, prudish, shy or just tense up. Sometimes a bit of fun can help the situation. Why not give your sexual parts names and give them characters of their own. If 'Pussy' or 'Fanny' is off sex, it is not your fault. Similarly, if 'Willie' or

'Johnny' cannot manage to perform, do not blame yourself. To help get over any fears or problems, these characters need looking after, encouraging and understanding. Talk about how they might feel, what they want and give them personalities. Maybe you want a wild sex life with your partner but feel you will not be respected. Blame it all on your sexual characters. It is their fault the sexual behaviour is outrageous, not yours.

Pretending you are someone else can make you feel sexier. You might want to keep your imaginary identity in your head or share the fantasy with your partner. Why not act out the fantasy together? You need not feel guilty about sex or feel your normal self-affected in any way. If you still find you have deep-seated problems, a sex counsellor will be able to help in most cases.

Unfortunately, on the films, the impression is often given that sex is always good. The man meets the woman, and in no time at all they are engaged in and enjoying sex. The woman immediately reaches a sexual climax and tells us in loud appreciation. Although often stimulating to watch, you may feel sex is not quite like that for you. This can cause feelings of inadequacy, or you may wonder why you or your partner does not respond in a similar way. A lot of women never reach a climax during intercourse. Some fake an orgasm as they think it is what is required. They might enjoy the experience and excitement of sex, but it is through understanding their own body that they can learn how to gain full sexual satisfaction. For some, stimulation on the clitoris may be the only way to get a climax. Sex toys or vibrators can help. Oral sex can bring pleasure for both men and women but mutual agreement is needed. Some men and women go from relationship to relationship seeking the sexual high depicted on films. Even if reached at the start of a relationship, unless worked at, the excitement can wear off when day-to-day normality sets in.

Sadly, for some young women they have had to experience female genital mutilation, a practice still performed in some countries. The removal of the clitoris takes away the woman's right to enjoy sexual climax and enjoyment. In some cases, the vagina is made narrower too. The operation is painful and can result in infection. Penetration during sex is possible but often painful and many women suffer all their lives. There is an active worldwide campaign to ban the practice, but religious customs and superstition take generations to change.

Sex, like the relationship, will have good and bad times. Sometimes you or your partner may not want to be close while other times you cannot get enough sex. You may find yourself thinking of other things or even other partners, fantasy or otherwise, while having sex. Your partner will not know, nor will you know what they are thinking. You may pretend you are enjoying yourself to satisfy your partner. Do you initiate sex or do you wait until your partner approaches you? What if your partner is not in the mood? How do you turn each other down without hurting or humiliating? Do you reassure your partner of your love? Be honest and try and understand your partner's feelings too. A meaningful relationship emotionally and sexually will result. Fantasy, dressing up, play-acting or imagination can stimulate sexual excitement and bring more fun into your love life. You can enjoy sex anywhere or anytime, as long as you both consent and use common sense.

Everyone has a 'Yuk' factor. Sexual experimentation is fun, but sometimes may go too far. If you or your partner finds something is distasteful, you have a right to say no. Opinions should be respected. There is no must, ought or should. Perhaps it is a sexual position, sex toys or even a sexy film you do not like. Maybe your partner wants others to join in the sexual activity. Discuss the situation and hopefully understanding will result. Sex is between consenting adults. Getting older does not mean that your sex life ceases. If you do want to stop sex activity as you age, it is important that both partners accept the situation. There are creams to help if dryness is a problem. Communication at this time is essential. It is so sad when misunderstanding or complacency leads to an affair.

Some men and women think everything about sex is distasteful. It could be the result of strict upbringing or a bad experience. Maybe body image is preventing you from having a relationship. The idea of touching your own private parts or those of others can cause distress. The mess of ejaculation, the sounds and smells of sex, together with the worry of pregnancy, AIDS or other sexual diseases can cause barriers to a full sex life. An understanding partner or a sex therapist can help. If a disability is a problem, there is help available. Sex is not compulsory. Touching in other ways, cuddling and enjoying a feeling of being loved are important. A relationship can be enjoyed without sex and the chapter on relationships may help.

The opportunity to enjoy your sexuality with a partner is not always possible. Some single people long for sex while others are pleased that they do not have to participate. There is no law against masturbation or stimulation by sex toys. There are a lot of magazines, books and internet sites which can enhance sexual excitement. The use of pornography can be quite controversial, but judging from the use of pornographic sites on computers, it is very much part of internet life. Prostitution is controversial too. It is a criminal offence when anyone is forced into sexual activity against their will. Sadly, this happens all over the world. Without more sexual education and understanding, unwanted sex will continue to be an evil in society.

Exercise (iii) Enhance Your Sex Life

Sort out the contraception.

Cleanliness is important, why not shower or bath together. Soap each other down.

Try new underwear or nightwear, or dress up to be someone else or swap clothes. Try animal masks, wear hats, wigs, sexy shoes, or anything that brings a bit of fun.

Use perfumes, creams or edible spreads.

A light meal, music, alcohol (in moderation), a sexy film. Feed each other. Eat in the nude, dance to the music.

Try a foot massage, tickle each other or gently chastise.

Use sex toys or improvise – anything that is not going to do harm but enhance the experience.

Have sex in every room in the house. Don't forget the car and the garage.

Sex on the floor, against the wall, on the table, desk etc.

Make love with a paper bag over your head or blindfolded, or with your ears blocked.

Try different positions. Act innocent, wild or domineering.

Lighting full on or off.

Have sex in front of a mirror.

Bedroom decor can give atmosphere. Make a tent with bedclothes for a secret hideaway.

What about sex in a cupboard?

If you are concerned about the mess or soiling anywhere, lay a towel down and keep tissues handy. Be imaginative, as long as you both agree and it is safe and legal.

CHAPTER FOUR — YOUR BODY MATTERS

Do you feel fit? What about your diet, smoking or drinking? Are you looking after yourself? When was the last time you touched your toes or did any knee bends? Most of us find it difficult to motivate ourselves. There are many reasons why not to exercise. There is not enough time in the day, you do not like gyms, you have tried but failed, and who cares anyway? Are these excuses familiar? Maybe it is the time to reassess your lifestyle. Despite all the warnings about obesity, heart disease or lack of mobility, it is easy to think it will be other people who have health problems. Apart from keeping fit, keeping check on different areas of your body is important. Do you check for lumps, examine moles or attend health checks when asked to go? What about your blood pressure or cholesterol? You only have one life and one body, look after it.

DIET

Very few people are very satisfied with their bodies. It is not always easy to eat the right things. Being overweight is because we are all eating too much. How many diets have you tried? They rarely work and the weight returns plus some more. The only answer is to cut down. Strict diets never work long-term, despite the initial loss of weight. Using smaller plates, only one helping and eating slowly does help.

The following eating theory might give you a new understanding. You probably remember at school how we all learnt about the camel. When it has to go on a trek, it fills its hump with food to be able to cope with the deprivation as it crosses the desert. Our bodies seem to react much the same. When you go on an extreme diet, you deprive your body of food. As soon as you stop, the body decides it is not going to be caught out like that again. It stores even more food just in case. If your body has regular small meals, you will find you lose weight. It works like clockwork. Like any machine, the body requires the right fuel, proteins, vitamins, fats, carbohydrates, etc. in moderation. The food goes in, the nutrients are used up and the residue expelled. Once in a regular eating pattern, your body will have no need to store. Don't get the hump by dieting, just cut back on food.

Comfort eating can often be a problem. Loneliness, a bereavement, or boredom can be the cause. Have you gorged on chocolate, demolished a packet of biscuits or stuffed yourself with crisps or chips? Having eaten, you feel bad, and then eat even more to compensate. Similarly, excess smoking or drinking is used as a crutch. A lot of people binge. At certain times you might raid the cupboard for anything. Handfuls of cereals, currants, packets of biscuits, anything will do. There is this terrible urge to eat. This is quite normal and in a woman is usually connected to the menstrual cycle. Try drinking a glass of water and then eating a slice of bread with no spread or butter. It may stop the craving and prevent you eating very fattening things. So many food scares come and go, but despite the gloom and doom, most people live a lot longer than previous generations. Unfortunately, recent obesity statistics predict that this may not be the case for much longer.

EATING DISORDERS

When bingeing is a regular or daily occurrence, there is a problem. You may hide your problem by making yourself sick. Maybe you put on more and more weight. Alternatively, your problem might be the opposite. Do you refuse food? Have you made yourself anorexic? Admit it to yourself. Do others know about your disorder or are you keeping it secret? There is a lot of help and information available. See the chapter on mental illness.

Contrary to popular belief, most disorders are not about weight but about control. Perhaps your life has gone wrong. Things may have happened that you did not like but could do nothing about. Others around you might have been dictating your actions or pressurized you to behave in a way contrary to how you feel. Do your parents or a partner have unrealistic expectations as to how you should behave or achieve? Maybe you have put the expectations on yourself. Have you been humiliated or abused? Sometimes as your body becomes more sexy you may feel out of control. Unwanted sexual attention may be disturbing. The one area you can control is what you put into your mouth. For some it is a way to avoid growing up or taking on adult relationships. You may have the impression that to be thin brings happiness and riches. What is it that might have been the initial catalyst for your problem?

Once your controlled eating becomes an addiction, problems start. Warnings of consequences or dire threats do not make any difference. Families are often distraught as no one seems to be able to get answers. This cycle of eating is difficult to stop. The cure has to come from you, but you may not know how to change your habit. There is a great deal of help available. Get help with what you are doing before it is too late.

ALCOHOL

We live in a drinking culture. Booze is freely available and is something we can enjoy. The problem comes when drinking is taken to excess.

How often do you wish you had been less indulgent or wonder what you did while under the influence of alcohol? To some this is a regular occurrence and part of the social scene. Are you an alcoholic? The commonly held idea of an alcoholic is a down-and-out rolling round the street with a bottle in his hand. In fact, many people are alcoholics and do not realise their predicament. They might say, 'I can go without a drink for days and therefore I am not hooked'. The snag comes when they start drinking, they cannot stop. It is just one drink that is the catalyst. A need for alcohol kicks in and is uncontrollable. Get help if you recognise these traits.

FITNESS

Do you take fitness to extremes or have you just given up? A moderate amount of exercise — doing something you enjoy, is the ideal. Unless you are aiming for Olympic medals, there is no need to let exercise dominate your life. Stretching is one of the best therapies. Walk rather than ride. Take the stairs rather than the lift. You know if you feel fit or not. It is up to you. There are plenty of sports clubs, fitness centres or classes to help. Why not join a walking group, a dance class or kick-boxing? There is such a lot of activity out there. A lot of people join health clubs with the best intentions, but attendance only lasts a few weeks. Is that you? Why not try at home.

Ten minutes each morning of gentle stretching and exercise will make a big difference. Perhaps a friend will join a class with you, giving you an incentive.

ILLNESS

Unfortunately, despite all you may do to look after yourself, illness can strike. Have you had serious childhood illnesses, born with a disability or inherited a problem? Perhaps an accident or physical attack has caused long-term harm. Maybe you have had to cope with operations, long spells away from home in hospital or need looking after permanently. Mental illness, drug or alcohol addiction or a brain problem may change your personality. Have you got fertility problems or have to face cancer treatment? Anything that goes wrong can cause great distress. Career prospects, life plans or holidays have to be put on hold or abandoned.

Some cope remarkably well with illness. It does not mean that you do. You may feel sadness, anger and resentment because of past treatment, accidents, or disabilities. This can cause feelings of inadequacy as you grieve over the person you might have been. Loss of mobility, sight or hearing can be hard to accept. Scarring, hair loss, skin problems and anything that affects what you look like can make you feel different about yourself. There is a lot of help offered if you ask. Do not suffer alone.

Discovering a new lump, unexplained change of bowel function or unusual bleeding could be a warning or a problem, and it is important to seek medical advice. Dismissing these signs could make the situation worse. A doctor will advise you or put your mind at rest. Most things can be treated if caught early enough. Often you imagine the worst when there is nothing to worry about. You might think you will die, wonder how the family will manage, cry over the loss of time and start tidying cupboards. Negative thoughts are natural at times. We all have to face up to the fact that we are mortal and will die one day.

You might start to question what life is all about. Who are you? Why are you here? Is there a God? What happens when you die? It may give you a chance to reassess your life. Imagine you did die. How will you be remembered? Would you want to be buried or cremated? Would you want lots of flowers at your funeral? Some people plan their own funerals, choose the hymns and write their own obituary. Thoughts about your own death or those of others is normal.

Are you worried about going into hospital? Not knowing what will happen, being away from home or facing an operation, can all be reasons for concern. Perhaps you cannot wait to get medical matters sorted. Once there, nurses and doctors will do their best to reassure you. It is their job to get you well again and they will do all they can to do so. Being with strangers in a ward is not always easy. Others can have bad habits or be noisy or difficult. Loss of privacy may be a problem. You might make new friends. You will probably have weepy days, particularly after an anaesthetic. If you are not in control of bodily functions it can cause embarrassment and you may lose some inhibitions as a result. What sort of patient are you? Friends and family will no doubt visit. Rest and get well soon.

THE ILLNESS OF FAMILY OR FRIENDS

It may not be you who has to face illness, but a friend or member of your family. Accidents and illness can strike at any age. It can be heart-breaking while you watch someone you love going through a difficult time. Babies or children suffering can be particularly harrowing. If it is your partner or parent, there may be all sorts of fears. Will they be the same? How will you cope? There may be feelings of guilt or inadequacy. You may worry about showing your inner pain. The illness might only be temporary, but you imagine the worst. It is not a bad thing to think about how you would cope if something did go really wrong. The chapter on bereavement may help. Do you have to be a carer? Can you cope? Even the best of carers will have times of frustration. Tempers can get frayed with the demands on your energy and time.

When a parent is ill, you may find you swap roles and become the parent yourself. It can be made more difficult if there is a personality change. Irritating habits may get you down. Grief, guilt, duty and love get mixed up as you lose the person you knew. Do you put them in a home? What about the costs? A time might come when you have no option. There are so many problems when you least want them. It can be bewildering and frightening. You may pray for their release from suffering. Say what you want to say before it is too late.

Exercise (iv) Happiness chart

Look back and try and remember feelings over the years. We do not stay the same as we face what time throws at us. Your health and that of others can affect your happiness. Events in your life can affect both health and happiness too. Are you suffering a difficult time at the moment? It is so hard to imagine things will get better but they will. The following charts might help you understand about life. We are all on a roller coaster ride. Some people never experience emotional extremes in their life, while others yo-yo between highs and lows. No one has a perfect life.

Why not draw your own happiness chart to see how life has treated you?

Happiness is shown one to ten down the side of the chart. Number one being extremely happy and number ten feeling very low or suicidal. Life events are shown as pointers 'a to g', and the age at the time is shown along the bottom line.

Example: thirty-three-year old woman

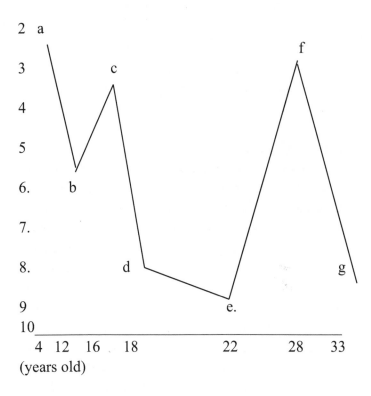

1

2   a

3   c   f

4

5

6.   b

7.

8.   d   g

9   e.

10
    4 12 16 18   22   28 33
(years old)

    a. Junior school
    b. Bullied at senior school
    c. college
    d. failed exams

e. unemployed
f. married, baby
g. postnatal depression

Example: twenty-six- year old man

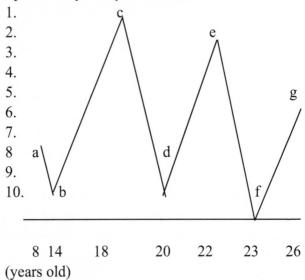

1.
2.
3.
4.
5.
6.
7.
8
9.
10.

8 14   18   20   22   23   26
(years old)

a. never felt loved
b. parents split
c. met first partner
d. broke up
e. new job
f. climbing accident
g. new relationship

CHAPTER FIVE — IMAGE AND HOW OTHERS SEE YOU

SELF-ACCEPTANCE

Have you had a good look at yourself recently? Do you like what you see? Very few people are totally satisfied with their body image. It is so easy to feel inadequate when we are swamped with photographically enhanced pictures, or read of people who seem to have it all. A great deal of stress can be caused in trying to be someone you are not. Pressure from a partner to dress in a certain way or the desire to keep up with friends or colleagues can cause problems both emotionally and financially. Confidence is built from acceptance of who you are, faults and all. Do you hide behind baggy or unflattering clothes in an attempt not to be noticed? Alternatively, do you go to great lengths to pretend you are confident, extremely sexual or very popular? Body piercing, tattoos, extreme hair dye or heavy make-up may be used to get attention away from who you really are.

You might not be blessed with good looks, but making the most of what you have is important. A friendly nature, pleasant personality or sense of humour shines through. It does not mean you should give up on appearance. A slovenly, don't care attitude will not enhance relationships, improve job prospects or increase pride in yourself. Film stars or rich people might spend thousands having face lifts, tummy tucks, hair transplants or breast enhancements, but it does not necessarily bring happiness. Most of us are stuck with what we have. There are advantages and disadvantages for every size and shape. If you are obviously very different and get noticed, it can be disturbing, but can also be turned to your advantage. Hundreds of people seek fame and notoriety, but you have it without trying. People go on TV doing strange things, pull faces for competitions, do daredevil stunts or eat grotesque things just to be noticed.

Being born attractive can be a great advantage, but for some it is a burden. You may not be taken seriously. Perhaps you are just seen as an object of desire. You may hate the sexual attention you attract and find it difficult to cope. Instead of enjoying your sexuality, aggression or laddish behaviour may be displayed, expressing hidden anger. Alternatively, shyness and embarrassment may prevent social contact. Try and think differently. Enjoy the attention; give them a smile if you like. You have it, they want it. What power! Any unwanted sexual harassment, stalking or touching is totally unacceptable. You must get help if you feel used or abused in any way.

MAKING THE MOST OF YOURSELF

Start from the beginning. Get a magnifying mirror and examine your face. Look at all the lines, discolouration and imperfections. Get to know your face. Consider what you want to do with any stray hairs. Is your skin very dry or greasy? If you wear makeup, check you have not missed bits or overdone any area. Similarly, get to know your body. Stand in front of a mirror and be honest about what you see. Most of us refuse to recognise the good points and only take note of the bad. Learn to love your body. Starting from the basic facts, you have to build up. The first point is cleanliness. Do you keep yourself clean, wash your hair regularly and use deodorant? Being fresh can make a lot of difference in how you feel. Smelling good can lift your spirits too. Do you keep your toe nails and finger nails clean? Feet are extremely important. Any bunions, painful areas or problems need to be dealt with as they make a difference to how you walk. Have you had an eye test recently? Do you need new glasses with more up-to-date frames? Bad teeth should be seen to. When was the last time you went to the dentist? A nice smile can work wonders.

Your hair can be your crowning glory. A good hairdresser or barber can give you advice and help to make the best of yourself. Do you have any skin problems? There are so many products on the market; there is no excuse not to make some attempt. You can get ideas from magazines, or ask at a chemist or department store if you need help. What about your eyebrows? Do they need some attention? Being a busy person or just getting older can make you forget about your image and take less care. It is so easy to feel like a blob. Build up your self-esteem and enjoy being you. What about your clothes? Are they all old-fashioned and boring? Do you need the reassurance of designer labels or try to copy a friend? Get all your clothes out on the bed and start sorting. Everything you have not worn for years should go out. Reassess what you have. Sort out anything that might need cleaning. Check buttons, zips or hems and do any repairs. Try things on and see if they still fit. There is no point in keeping things just in case you slim. Remember to keep some 'scruff wear' for gardening, painting or any dirty jobs. Experiment with different colour combinations. Sort out your accessories. What about your shoes? Chuck out any that are never worn or hurt your feet. Clean and polish others. Make sure you have enough coat hangers and replace things in your wardrobe in a different order. Drawers should be emptied and sorted too. When was the last time you bought any underwear? Buy some that makes you feel good, comfortable and sexy. Excess shopping for clothes can be used by some to cover up boredom, anxiety or stress. On the other hand, a bit of retail therapy can be a great boost to morale.

PRESENTATION

Deportment is very important. If you walk tall, it gives an air of confidence. Do you slouch or look down all the time? Perhaps you hang back and wait for others to do things. Shyness can be very difficult. No one is confident in every situation in life. Your demeanour can influence how people see you. How often do you give the wrong impression? You may be seen as a snob, when you are just shy. Maybe you talk too much, covering up insecurity. Being friendly and giving a smile can help considerably. Some turn to alcohol to gain confidence but this can lead to regrettable behaviour. Don't hide behind your mobile phone or text rather than see people face-to-face. People want to see you, get to know you and enjoy your company. Do you give the impression you are pleased to see them too?

This illustration might help you build confidence. Imagine a puppy coming into a room. He might be wagging his tail and obviously pleased to see you. You may react by patting it, perhaps talking to it and making a fuss. On the other hand, imagine the same puppy walking in and slinking into a corner. It takes a brave person to go over to see it. The dog may growl or bite. Perhaps it will reject your advances, or attack.

Which puppy is more like you? Confidence comes as you go out more and face the world. The world will not come to you.

Going for a job interview can be daunting. Get as much information about the firm beforehand. Arrive in good time and dress appropriately. Don't forget the employer will probably want to make a good impression too. A smile and good manners will enhance your chances. If asked, do not be afraid to talk about your qualities and what you have on offer. Remember, if you are turned down, the reasons could be endless, not a personal snub. You may be too confident or not confident enough. Employers may want someone with more experience or less, or possibly may feel that you might not cope, not giving you a chance. Think what they have missed by not employing you. Better luck next time.

We make many relationships in life, all with the potential to enhance or possibly damage our lives. We have relationships with various friends, brothers, sisters, parents, grandparents, relatives, work colleagues, partners, children and others. Some are thrust upon us and others chosen. There is a lot of truth in the saying, 'You choose your friends but not your relations'.

FRIENDS OR RELATIONSHIPS

Do you have difficulty making friends? Maybe a past bad experience or feelings of inadequacy prevent a relationship developing. What sort of friend do you want? Friends can be so many things to different people. They do not have to be close, knowing your inner most secrets and sharing your life. Just having one friend can be very supporting, but hurtful if things go wrong. A collection of different friends is ideal. Enjoy people's company for what they offer and ignore their faults. Perhaps you enjoy someone's sense of humour but don't like their morals. Maybe you appreciate their artistic talents, their intellect, or you share a love of dogs. How often have you expected a friend to provide everything and felt let down? When friendship is returned, it is a bonus not a right. Friends can be very important if you have a crisis in your life. A card or phone call can be very comforting. Do not expect anything. Not everyone is able to assist or recognise your plight when things go wrong. They might have busy lives and genuinely not have time. Maybe they are not the caring type and avoid emotion of any kind. Some may be waiting for you to ask for help and are worried about being intrusive.

Meeting people is not always easy. How much time do you have to socialize? Speaking on chat lines, texting or emailing helps some, but a face-to-face encounter is by far the best. Evening classes, clubs, interest groups, churches, sports centres etc. all give opportunities to meet people. Why not take part in community projects, charities or participate in a fun run or sponsored walk? Get out more. Smile and be friendly. People will introduce you to other people and so your circle of acquaintances, and ultimately friends, will grow and grow. Friends, like any other relationship, have to be cultivated. How often do you arrange to meet up? Do you remember birthdays, ring or text occasionally? No one wants to be swamped. Knowing someone thinks of you and enjoys your company occasionally, makes you feel good. Friends do come and go. They can move out of your life for all sorts of reasons. It can be hurtful or sad. We all change, grow up, move house, lose contact or just grow apart. Some sadly die, shaking your life foundations.

Are you waiting to meet that perfect person? Maybe you feel inadequate and dwell on your own faults. How often do you feel not attractive enough, not intelligent enough, not fit enough, or uninspiring? In other words, you are expecting perfection in yourself. Perfect people often expect perfect relationships and a perfect life. There is no such thing. Look at what you can offer in life instead. In most areas, being good enough is sufficient. We all have faults. You may have mood swings, be quite easily irritated or self-doubting at times. Do you feel pressure to look young, be rich or fit? Both men and women worry about their image. Some imagine the opposite sex wants perfection. We are bombarded by images on the screen of ideal.

WORK COLLEAGUES

You may have to spend eight hours each day in the company of others. Perhaps you enjoy the company of your work colleagues. They may be people you like, or hate. Remember, they have problems in their lives too. Colleagues may be from totally different backgrounds, have different habits and manners or have strange attitudes to life. In a job you have to try and relate while you work together, but disputes and misunderstanding often occur. Do you have problems with people in authority? Is your boss understanding or corrupted by power? Competition and expectations can enhance advancement in a firm or, alternatively, cause tension, insecurity or despair. The money may be the only reason you stay in your job. Do you feel trapped? Perhaps a relationship at work has gone wrong. Getting too close with work colleagues can cause problems. There is more than hurt pride at stake if you break up. Maybe your work colleagues are your only friends. You may have little time to socialize outside the working environment. Difficulties may come with retirement or redundancy. Leaving work can leave a big gap in your life with no one to talk to without making an effort. Work may give you status in society or make you feel needed. Would you feel vulnerable or worthless without a job? Having interests and friends outside the work environment can help considerably. A whole new and exciting world waits.

Exercise (v) Special people in your life
What support do you have in life, if any, and who is most important to you? Write down numbers one to five. If the person closest to you is put at number one, who would you include at the other numbers? If you have experienced a loss of a loved one, perhaps you could include them too. The following will give you some idea.

Here are some examples:

1. Partner	1. Mother	1. Child
2. Mother	2. Children	2. Partner
3. Brother	3. Partner	3. Grandmother (deceased)
4. Girlfriend	4. In-laws	4. Father
5. Sister	5. Friend	5. Mother

Everyone's emotional support is so different. It is not always the person you expect who is the closest. There may be some surprises. The list may illustrate your loneliness or difficulty in making relationships.

It might show up problems with parents, partners or children. No one is judging. You will know if things are not how you would like them to be. If you have a partner, get them to do a list too. Where would you like to be on their list?

CHAPTER SIX-MENTAL HEALTH

The recent rise in mental health is alarming. Many people are diagnosed each year with some form of mental illness, and doctors are continually being faced with patients suffering with anxiety or depression. Even more worrying is the number of children presenting with symptoms of mental illness. Many young people are coping with mental problems too, but for various reasons, fail to acknowledge any difficulties. The delay in treatment can make matters worse. Maybe life is too busy, exams are looming, or you are just too scared as to what might be wrong. If you find yourself struggling, there is help available. It is not a failure to ask.

There have been huge advances in diagnosis and treatment in recent years, but unfortunately mental health is still not getting the recognition it needs. More and more famous people are now acknowledging their problems with the illness, which in turn helps others to confront their own difficulties. There is some new exciting research being done, apparently, revealing that there may be a link between the mind and inflammation in the body. This will open up new understanding and may help in some areas of mental health in the future.

Depression is very common and medically recognized as a condition needing intervention. There are different types of depression and degrees of severity. See a doctor if you are finding difficulty in functioning properly, making daily tasks impossible. Feeling down, anxious or tearful at times is normal, but if your symptoms have gone on for some time, you need to get help. Are you suffering from dramatic mood swings? A great sense of euphoria followed by deep depression can dominate your life. These may be a sign of manic depression, sometimes called bipolar, and there is help available. You may be taught how to manage your moods, avoid situations that make things worse and learn how to cope when confronted with stress. Medication might help and your doctor or medical practitioner will advise.

After having a baby, post-natal depression can follow. It is no sign of failure. Coping with the baby or showing any bonding, care or love is sometimes impossible. Your own expectations and those of other people may add to your distress. Feeling a bit down after having a baby is common, but if this goes on for weeks, you need help. Men and women can both suffer post-natal depression, and it can happen anytime, usually during the first year. You may feel sad, lack energy or find making decisions difficult. You may not want to socialize, and despite feeling lonely, feel frightened to face the world. Get help. Your emotions are understood.

Sometimes the weather or season can have an effect on mental health. SAD or seasonal affective disorder creates difficulties, particularly during the winter months. Feeling extreme tiredness, anxiety or complete lack of motivation can be very hard if you are trying to keep a job or looking after family. Friends or family may notice and suggest you see a doctor. Accepting something is wrong is often the most difficult time. Be honest with your doctor as to how you really feel. Once cared for by the medical profession, everything will be done to get you better.

There are many types of other mental illnesses, eating disorders, addictions, personality disorders, thought disorders and mood disorders. Any of these can ruin your life unless help is accepted. Your studies, relationships, work or day-to-day living can be a great struggle as you try and cope with unwanted emotions. There is no shame in asking for help, even if you are not sure that the matter is serious. The exercise at the end of the chapter will help you recognize symptoms. If you are concerned and feel either you or someone else is in immediate physical danger, you should call the emergency services. The police and ambulance people are very familiar with the procedure and will guide you through the situation.

You may be diagnosed with schizophrenia. If you find it difficult to understand reality, are confused in your thinking and possibly hear voices, you need help. Schizophrenia covers a wide range of symptoms and severity. It can happen quite suddenly or evolve over some time. It is a complete myth that everyone with schizophrenia is dangerous. Similarly, having schizophrenia does not mean you have a split personality. It is a mental condition which is suffered differently by each individual, covering a range of behaviour. Your background, environment, health, diet and attitude to life can all have a part to play in how your symptoms present. Drug abuse has been recognized as a possible cause in some people. Chemical imbalance in the brain is considered the main problem and medical intervention is needed to try and get equilibrium.

A PSYCHOTIC ATTACK

This is much more than a panic attack and is a sign of illness. You may collapse on the floor, cry uncontrollably or howl like an animal. There can be a feeling of terror or losing your mind. Hearing voices or seeing things increases the stress. It is not easy for a bystander to comprehend, and the symptoms are often mistaken for a fit or heart attack. See a doctor. Individuals already on treatment can be affected too, and assurance should be sought from the medical profession.

DIAGNOSIS OF MENTAL ILLNESS AND TREATMENT

A doctor will analyse your situation and consider what is appropriate for your condition. In some cases talking therapy is recommended. Difficulties, anxieties and emotions are discussed with a counsellor or therapist experienced in dealing with your problems. It is often a great relief to talk to someone who understands, and they will help guide you through coping strategies and new understandings. You may need medication which could be in injection, tablet or liquid form. The medication is likely to be ongoing, with regular checks to see how you are getting on. Sometimes blood tests are needed, and in some cases scans are used to detect any physical problems. If your doctor feels that a referral to the mental health team would be beneficial, an appointment will be made for you to see a psychiatrist. Decisions will be made regarding your further treatment. Some medication may require careful monitoring and being in a mental health ward allows easier observation. Doing as the doctor suggests is very important as your recovery depends on it.

If serious mental illness is suspected, your doctor or counsellor will refer you to the mental health team where you will be seen by a psychiatrist or psychologist. There are different outcomes for different diagnoses. You may be given medication, offered therapy or asked to attend a day clinic for observation. On the other hand, if your situation is more complex, you may be sent to a mental health hospital.

There are two types of wards or units, secure units and semi-secure. The secure unit is for people who are a danger either to themselves or someone else. There are usually two locked entrance doors for safety reasons. Everyone entering must make sure they have no sharp items, plastic bags or anything that could be used to harm. The other mental units usually have only one locked door, monitored by reception staff. Once there, in most cases, you would be allocated your own bedroom with a cupboard and your own bathroom. It would depend on the accommodation available. The staff in these units are very understanding and helpful and will do all they can to get you better.

In the case of an acute mental breakdown, you may be detained in hospital with an order, agreed by two doctors and other members of the mental health team. If your nearest relative is concerned about your behaviour and feels hospital is the best place for you, they can be influential in having you confined to the hospital too, but not before a form is filled in and two doctors agree that you are reacting or behaving in such a way that detention in hospital would be beneficial. There are different levels of confinement, depending on the seriousness of the situation or where you are in your treatment, enabling the mental health doctors to have power over certain aspects of your life. They take the responsibility for your assessment and can give you treatment, even if you do not want it or believe it to be unnecessary. You cannot discharge yourself without the agreement of the medical team. The police can be involved if someone goes missing. It can be challenged legally, and there are management meetings and tribunals regularly to assess that any actions by mental health doctors are appropriate, and that your feelings are known. Your nearest relative may be able to apply for you to be discharged, but the approved mental health professional can block the decision if they think it unreasonable.

For some, sadly, suicide is seen as the answer and the only way out of their situation. Men are more likely to take their own life than women, but suicides of both sexes have increased in recent years. Suicide is discussed in the chapter on bereavement. Would you see the signs of mental illness in yourself or in others? There are as many different forms of mental illness and the symptoms can vary accordingly. Some people have more than one disorder at the same time.

There is so much still to understand about mental illness, but new treatments are enabling people to recover well and lead productive lives.

Exercise (vi) Mental Health Concerns
Do you or someone else suffer a mental health problem? Look through the list below, and if you feel there is a concern, get help.
Unable to concentrate, lost ability to reason or do calculations
Find socializing really difficult and would rather avoid it
Seeing things
Hearing things
Worrying excessively about exams
Debilitating stress and hopelessness
Not eating, losing excessive weight
Overeating to excess to feed your concerns
Twitching, moving strangely, talking nonsense
Feeling rejected and persecuted by society
Having delusions of grandeur or supernatural powers
Imagine you are someone else
Feeling violent towards people or yourself.
Scared you may carry it out
Uncontrollable swearing or anger
Not sleeping
Pushing yourself to exhaustion
Excessive fears, worries or anxiety
Spending money recklessly

Giving away everything without any thought
Serious self-harm
Suicidal attempts

GET HELP – YOUR PROBLEMS ARE
UNDERSTOOD

CHAPTER SEVEN —
UNDERSTANDING YOUR PARENTS

As you get older you may find yourself wondering why your parents think like they do. Do you recognise them as individuals in their own right, with feelings and problems? What was life really like for them when they were young? Have you ever thought what pressures they might have had from their parents or from the society they lived in. Ask them now, before it is too late.

Parents do not necessarily have parenting skills. No one gives lessons. Most parents just do their best. Do you appreciate their input in your upbringing or are you glad to be out of their clutches? Everyone's relationship with parents is different. Perhaps you have step-parents or were brought up by someone else in the family. Did you get on with those in the parental role or has the relationship always been difficult? Some people rely on parents too much. Do you idolize one of them or take sides in their relationship? Parents' perceptions, opinions and morals may be different to yours. Modern ideas can be difficult to understand and the pace of life too fast. Have you considered what it is like to be them?

Parents can find it difficult as youth drifts away. They probably still feel very young inside and never expected to be in the situation they are in now. There may be a specific birthday or event that triggers off these feelings. It can be the time for them to reassess life and consider the future. Is there any romance left? What about work? Have they reached their personal potential or is it still to come? Maybe they want a change of direction in a career or more free time to enjoy other pursuits. Looks may have changed over the years. Complexions might not be so smooth and the body beginning to be affected by gravity. Is the weight piling on and fitness a problem? Perhaps energy levels have declined. They may never now have that lead role in a film, be a pop star or become managing director. Accepting these disappointments is not always easy. There is some consolation though. They do not have to cope with the trials and tribulations of youth.

Middle age is the time when some parents start to look back and wonder where the time has gone. They may reminisce and tell you of how things used to be. They begin to wear things for comfort rather than create an impression. High heels may not be the most important thing in a woman's wardrobe. Underwear that pulls in the bulges, or sensible bras might replace the saucy outfits as sexual feelings change. Men are the same. The old jacket and trousers come out yet again, and those slippers are so comfortable. They are not past it yet though. They may have more than forty years to live. Life expectancy goes up and up. What now? They can still have a lot of fun. When did you last have a good laugh together? Make the most of the time you have with them, and the wisdom and experience they have gained in life.

What sort of parents have you got? Do they have a lot to do with you and your family, always welcoming and available to help or babysit. Alternatively, do they like to keep their distance? Perhaps they resent the mess caused by children, have a very busy life or just want to be by themselves. Do you expect them to be there for you and keep up with all that is going on with your life? Maybe they do not have much of a life and live life through you, continually questioning your movements. For some parents, loneliness and isolation can be a problem if there are no friends or interests. Do they make this your problem too? Perhaps you are still living at home. Financial considerations may make living alone difficult. What about freedom, both theirs and yours? Living under their rules can cause friction and there have to be compromises.

As people get older, sometimes memory seems to go. It is difficult to remember someone's name or the title of a book. It happens to everyone. If you think about all the things the brain has absorbed over the years, it is not surprising a few things are forgotten. It may be the time to start writing lists. A grocery list kept in the kitchen may help. Any item that has run out or is needed can be added at the time you think about it, making a trip to the supermarket easier. A different list kept by the telephone can be a great help too. As people get older they often worry more. Having had experience of life, they are more aware of what can go wrong. Are you giving them reason to worry? Exams, staying out late, the problems of career choice, gap years, university or college entrance, all add stress. Your choice of partner, your financial situation and your health may cause them to make a fuss. If there are grandchildren, the way you bring them up may be different. Do you appreciate their input or resent the interference?

LEAVING WORK

Retirement may be thrust upon your parents or be their choice. Ill health, redundancy or being unable to find a job may force an early retirement. For some, bitterness, anger or depression can result as they grieve the loss of lifestyle and feel not wanted. They may miss work colleagues, suffer from loss of identity and be thoroughly bored. For many, retirement cannot come soon enough. Your parents may be able to do all those things they dreamed of. There may be holidays, hobbies, sports, new interests and new people to meet. They will have time to enjoy the grandchildren, see friends, travel or fix the house.

Perhaps they want to learn a new skill, read more, listen to more music or get fit.

A move to a cheaper property might be necessary. Romantic ideas of living by the sea or going abroad to live do not always work out or bring the happiness hoped for, but can be a challenge for some. Perhaps they move nearer you. Is that what you wanted or were you not consulted? Do you resent them spending the money or enjoying themselves while you struggle to make ends meet? Maybe it is the opposite as they struggle to cope, trying to avoid spending the money they hope to leave in their will. Guilt, resentment, jealousy or greed can so often be triggered by these issues.

We all have to die one day. In most cases it will be your parents who die before you. Health can become a major topic of conversation as parents get older. People around them begin to fall to various ailments or die. The menopause, prostate problems, back pain or just general stiffness remind them that youth is slipping away. One of your parents may be facing the future alone. Are you expected to be there for them, visit regularly or do anything they ask? Maybe you enjoy the caring role and feel you want to do all you can to help. Alternatively, you may resent the interference in your life. Perhaps you do things because you feel it is your duty. There may be feelings of guilt while you struggle to balance time spent with your own family. Cooking for one is not easy, and they may crave your company. Sundays are often the most difficult days for someone who is on their own. Having a regular commitment to meet can cause problems. What would you be like if you were on your own at their age? Would you be able to cope? What if a parent seeks a new partnership? Romance or companionship is wonderful at any age. Maybe you rejoice in their new happiness. Alternatively, their choice may not be yours. You may resent the intrusion into your family or worry about inheritance.

THE LATTER YEARS

As old age approaches, life can still be enjoyed to the full. You may wonder how much longer they will be fit or what will happen when they are really old. It is the unknown that is difficult. Will they be mobile, be able to drive or even walk? What about incontinence? Will they be able to keep their independence, do the chores round the house and dress themselves? What about going senile or mental illness? We all ask these questions and worry, so do they. You may have to discuss with them about a residential place or nursing home if that is what they want. Roles may be reversed as you become a carer, taking on the responsibilities of their finance and housekeeping. It can be a time to encourage them to write their memoirs, put their finances in order and make a will. There may be extra costs as they have to pay for someone to help with housework or the garden. In some cases, social services have to get involved to enable them to have a good quality of life.

No one knows how long your parents will live. You may have expectations of inheritance money, but nursing home fees may eat into their savings. Perhaps you are not included in the will anyway. Death may be something they fear or look forward to. Similarly, you may dread their passing or long for them to go. Their quality of life might be very upsetting. They have a role to play even if they are bedridden. They are unique. Tell them what you want to say before it is too late. They may have been good or bad parents, but they are the only ones you have.

CHAPTER EIGHT — THE OPPOSITE SEX

It is not possible to understand another person totally, just as we can never fully know ourselves. Men may be lovable, sexy, frustrating, deceitful, annoying, considerate or selfish, all qualities women might possess too, but men are different. Years ago there was a TV programme showing little children's behaviour. Two little girls were put together in a room and watched, and similarly two boys in another room had their attitudes observed. The little girls talked, shared and generally related. The boys hardly spoke. They played individually and barely acknowledged the existence of each other. It could have been the children they chose. Some people think that men and women are primed to behave differently, and it all goes back to the animal kingdom. Male animals have to be extremely self-sufficient, guard their territory and be on the lookout for rivals. However, the recent programmes on wildlife show very different roles developed by different animals. It is often the female that goes out hunting, and the male looks after the offspring.

In the past, showing emotion was considered weakness for some men and still is, in some circles. After wars and disasters, a stiff upper lip was considered manly. There have been more men crying on TV recently, which must be very reassuring to many. Both men and women have the same vulnerability and should be allowed to express their feelings.

Have you ever thought about your own upbringing? The nursery rhyme tells us, girls are made of sugar and spice and all things nice, while boys are made of slugs and snails and puppy dogs' tails. Even if your parents tried hard not to stereotype sexual attitudes, girls and boys behave differently. Despite equality, most girls still love stories of romance, while boys read of adventure and war. In the past, nurturing and caring tendencies were considered more prevalent in girls, while rough physical activities are more likely with boys. Nowadays there are many opportunities for both sexes to be equal at school, on the sports field and in career choices. The subservient attitude instilled into girls of previous generations is over in most western societies. People grow up to have a healthy and responsible attitude to the opposite sex, accepting individuality.

Unfortunately, society is not perfect. Children learn about paedophiles, rapists, stalkers, gropers and people who spike drinks. It is usually men who are considered the culprits. Internet grooming too is an area of danger, where men use unsuspecting girls and boys to satisfy their sexual appetites. There may be more understanding of sexual exploitation, but sexual crimes will always be with us. Attitudes towards rape or any sexual attack are changing and victims are much more likely to be believed and action taken.

Being a young person in the computer age is exciting but can be dangerous. There is a lot of pornography and sexual content online, often giving a warped sense of what might be considered normal. Having the opportunity to send sexual photos to loved ones seems innocent enough, but photos can get into the wrong hands. Sexting, often practiced by underage children, can have a very unfortunate outcome. The computer has helped both sexes to understand sex, maturity and reproduction, perhaps much sooner than previous generations. There are warnings of unwanted pregnancy and the danger of AIDS and other sexually transmitted diseases. Sex is normal, but all the images and dangers can be very disturbing for some. Do you have overprotective parents, or maybe they do not seem to care? Perhaps there is a strong religious belief regarding sexuality. Everyone has their own attitude towards society and sex which can be positive or negative.

Are you homosexual or just feel different? For some, the awareness may happen when very young, while others only recognise feelings from sexual encounters. Being gender fluid is now accepted, as many people find it difficult to fit into a particular category of sexuality. Do you try to keep it all a secret? You may worry about rejection or ridicule if parents, a partner or friends knew. Admitting your feelings and coping with the consequences is not always easy, but there is often a great sense of relief. Be yourself. There are organisations to help if you need them. Marriage between similar-sex partners is now acceptable, many bringing up children in the relationship. All men have a feminine side, and women have a masculine side too, a fact some find very threatening.

The sex drive for each person is different. For most, there is a primitive drive to find a mate. The search can dominate your thoughts and actions for years. You may try to impress by the way you dress or the way you behave. Some men and women just want sex, while others are looking for a relationship. The physical attributes or sexual attitude of a person may spark a response, while with others, a sense of humour, a caring personality or a shared interest may be the attraction. It is a complete myth that all men want a fashion model. Women do not want a Mr. Universe either. Some men and women are very shy or frightened of the opposite sex. Romance can blossom through a long friendship or a chance encounter. There is no law as to who makes the first move. A woman might have a higher sex drive than a partner or enjoy being a sexual predator.

Women no longer need to wait for Prince Charming to arrive, but actively seek out companionship, if they want to. Many choose to be single, having seen the devastation of divorce. At dances, wall flowers are things of the past as women dance on their own if no man is available. Women can have their own careers, money and homes, seeking equality where possible. Single women can have babies from artificial insemination. The position men had in society has altered considerably, and some men find it difficult to find a role. Who cooks, who looks after the children, who does the DIY? These are all negotiable. Both men and women can have preconceived ideas how they want their partners to be. Ideas are often based on how their parents behaved. Judging from the high divorce rates, not many live up to expectations. For some men, being warm, dry and well fed is what they want from a relationship. The idea of picking up a duster, cleaning the floor or doing the ironing is quite foreign to them. Similarly, the expectations that women do the housework or cook are now regularly challenged. Do you accept this situation or is it a battlefield? There are no rules on male or female duties.

What about food? There is a lot of truth in the saying 'the way to a man's heart is through his stomach'. Wonderful exotic dishes may or may not be appreciated, but nursery food usually gets the compliments. Does he criticise your cooking because it is not like mum used to make? Some men love cooking, and some women hate it. Do you share the job or just get instant meals? The chore of everyday cooking can be very time-consuming and taken for granted. Is cleaning the kitchen and washing up afterwards a shared experience? Perhaps you go out to restaurants? Unfortunately, some consider this an extravagance and just for courting days. What about the shopping? Dragging a reluctant partner round the shops does not add to the enjoyment.

Most men and women need space away from each other. Work may mean time apart, or sport or hobbies take up evenings or weekends. Being left on your own while your partner is busy may not be what you want but is sometimes a necessity. Unless you have things to do while they are away, resentment can build up. Do you feel threatened by a night out with the girls or a stag weekend? Your insecurity may not be understood and only through communication can the problem be solved. Dominating someone and preventing them from pursuing interests can cause great conflict, but a balance usually can be found.

Power is very important to some men and women. They might hide behind success and status at work. Having a job gives an identity. There will be talk about sales figures, business takeovers, or the importance of a job, to give the impression they are better than the next person. For some, money and what it buys means everything. Are you keen to be seen as very successful? Perhaps your car gives you a position in society. The type of car you drive being of particular importance. A partner may be put under pressure to reflect your glory. How often do you dominate the conversation?

There are big changes over the last fifty years as to how men and women behave, or rather how they are expected to behave. Men being dominant are now not accepted. For years women have accepted sexual unwanted touching, comments and innuendo. The saying 'men will be men' allowed men to display all sorts of disgraceful behaviour. Women were often exploited and used, with nowhere to go to complain. The media has highlighted the abuse, but it will take a long time for some men to accept equality. Everyone is expected to respect the other person and control their own sexual desires. It will not stop parents worrying about girls going out scantily dressed. Have you thought through your ideas on the subject and how you react with the opposite sex?

Exercise (vii) People watching
This exercise helps to take you out of yourself and is a bit of fun. Find somewhere where you can watch people. It may be in a park, while standing in a queue, at an airport or on the bus.

(a) Notice what people wear. Imagine what they might have been thinking when they chose that outfit from their wardrobe. Are they trying to be noticed or perhaps the opposite? Are you conscious of how much you judge people, sexually, because of weight, religion or colour?

(b) What career do you think they have or have had in the past? Let your imagination run wild. Could they be a secret agent, an Olympic swimmer, a disc jockey, a bank manager or a rat catcher? You have no idea, but it is fun guessing. You can even build up a story around them.

(c) What do you think they are feeling? Perhaps they are grieving, stressed or sad. Alternatively, are they in love, won the lottery or just content?

(d) If they were playing the same game, what do you imagine they think you are?

(e) What do you imagine they think you are feeling?

CHAPTER NINE — RELATIONSHIP SURVIVAL

In buying a house the advice is 'location, location, location'. In a successful relationship the advice is ' communication, communication, communication'. Being able to talk to one another, being honest and open and ready to admit fault will stand you in good stead for the rest of your life. There is a saying that may help:

> If you are wrong... admit it,
> If you are right... SHUT UP.

You may choose to live apart, spending time together but enjoying your freedom. Living together may not be an option or something you do not choose to do before getting married. Before living together most people know each other quite well. It may turn out to be everything you hoped for and fulfils all your dreams. For some the outcome is unexpected. Is it your first time away from home? Perhaps homesickness is a problem and you miss your family. You may have previously been sharing a flat with friends where everyone helped with chores. Your partner may not be so accommodating. Maybe you had a place of your own and things were done your way. Discussing the expectations and difficulties will help the adjustment, but for some that adjustment is not easy.

Do you or your partner expect your lives to continue as usual and be free to come and go as before? Maybe one of you wants to 'settle down' while the other still wants the social scene. Is it your first time dealing with finance, cooking, washing or ironing? Budgeting for a household can be a challenge. Initially it can be a stormy time as expectation, ambitions or fantasies are shattered.

Where you live can influence how you feel. You may have to stay with in-laws or parents while the financial position improves. Not an easy situation with perhaps little or no privacy. Buildings are not always sound proof, and the idea of being heard in the bedroom might put you off showing affection. Possibly there are children in the home, and you are frightened of interruption. All these can cause stress. Did you both choose your home together? What about the decor? Do you both agree on colour and design? You may have moved into a partner's previous home. Are you allowed to change things?

In previous generations the allocation of chores, was more obvious. The woman did the household chores and the man went out to work. Nowadays it is not usually like that. Couples often both work. There may be shifts, long hours or other commitments. Are you the main bread winner? Perhaps you are both unemployed. Chores can become a source of disagreement. Who cleans the bath? Who does the ironing? How often do you change the bedclothes? The oven needs cleaning, the fridge defrosting, the rubbish put out and the windows cleaned. The list is endless. Who does what? Maybe you do it all. Resentment may build up over the years. It is sometimes easier to establish a regime from the beginning.

What about food and entertaining? Do you both enjoy cooking? Maybe you have very different food preferences. Friends may come round a lot. Do you like each other's friends? Have you got the same taste in music, TV soaps or films? A lot of this you may have found out beforehand, but there are usually some surprises.

During courting days, couples spend hours on the phone, texting each other and meeting whenever and wherever possible. Togetherness is important to give time to find out about each other, enjoy the closeness and experience all the joys of being a couple in love. Unfortunately, once together, people often feel there is no need for interactions any more, except perhaps in bed. The time for communicating is given less priority. Going out together, enjoying a walk, listening to each other and talking about feelings become less and less important. This in turn creates tensions, feelings of inadequacy, insecurity and resentment. Sex can become a weapon and a way to control. Unhappiness and discontentment creeps in. Money issues, the upbringing of children, in-laws, friends, outside interests, hobbies or work can all begin to create tensions. Without meaningful communication and understanding, the relationship can begin to flounder. Does any of this sound familiar?

A relationship can be illustrated in the form of a campfire. Initially, the couple tends it lovingly, adding fuel and making sure it is thriving. In this way they can enjoy the warmth, brightness and comfort that it gives out. Children thrive in this warmth too. Later a couple may be complacent. They are together now, and there is no need to bother any more. The result is the fire begins to go out — no warmth, no comfort and no joint purpose — the relationship begins to fail until there is no spark left.

Do you trust your partner? This can be very difficult for some, the insecurity often linked to past experiences. Perhaps there is an ex-partner causing problems. With open and honest communication, these difficulties can be overcome. Lies and secrets can increase feelings of betrayal as inevitably things get found out. Does your partner stop you from going out, seeing friends or visiting relatives? Jealousy is usually a sign of insecurity. With understanding, the feelings can improve. Unfortunately, for some partners it can develop into total possessiveness, and this sometimes needs outside help from a therapist or counsellor. No one should put up with any form of domestic violence or stay in a relationship because of fear. The chapter on abuse might help. Saying sorry can defuse many a volatile situation. It is not easy if you are both opinionated, but some couples thrive on rows and enjoy the challenge. To them a placid relationship would be boring.

Do you enjoy a close friendship with your partner? Perhaps you share everything and talk about things that have happened each day. Some never discuss work problems or discuss their past. This deprives their partner of knowing them and misunderstandings and wrongful perceptions can result. Make time to talk. It takes two people to talk their way into a relationship, and two people to keep it going. Expectations that a partner will solve all your problems are unrealistic. Everyone has bad days. There can be days when you may find it difficult to get motivated. Feelings of worthlessness can be overwhelming, or temper and moodiness seem uncontrollable. Accept your own moods rather than blame others. These feelings do not usually last long and have often gone by the next day unless there is an underlying depression.

Once you are in a relationship, you do not suddenly develop blinkers and only see each other. There are a lot of attractive people in the world. It is normal to notice but it does not mean that the relationship is threatened. Sensitivity should be used so that a partner is not made to feel inadequate. Other people will notice your partner, in the same way as you did, and similarly they will notice you. Enjoy the fact that you are attractive and appreciate others have assets too. A relationship has to be worked at, needing reassurance and stimulation. It should never be taken for granted. Keeping that spark alive is not always easy, but here are a few ideas.

Enjoy a candlelit dinner

Switch the television off for an evening and talk

Hold hands more

Go for a long walk together

Arrange a surprise — present, meal out, holiday

Enjoy a weekend away together

Ring up and say 'I love you'

Buy new underwear

Enjoy a picnic together

Go to a restaurant for breakfast

Try new sexual positions

Take more care of your appearance

Discuss what you would do if you won a lot of money

Get a new image

Do exercises together

Pray together

Go out and look at the stars together

Give each other a foot massage

Go dancing together

Do each other's hair

Get a romantic film or video

Watch a comedy
Get a new perfume/aftershave
Get fit
Talk about sex
Renew your vows
Listen to music you courted to
Visit old haunts
Tickle each other
Go back to the place where you met or married
Make a special meal
Put a loving note in a lunch box or under the pillow
Book into a hotel for the weekend and pretend you are on honeymoon
Find a hobby you can enjoy together
Say how good looking you partner is
Touch a lot more
Write a letter to each other

No partner owns the other. If you are always together, communication can become boring and any attempt to do anything solo can seem a threat. You both need space to be yourself and to develop personally. A relationship can be seen as two people walking a road. They are individuals connected by strings. For example, the memories string, the sex string, the trust string, the home string, the jokes string, the interests string and many more. If one string should break or get frayed, the others will hold the relationship together. Individually, you have your own path to follow too. What about your career, your fitness, your weight, your moods, habits or faith? These are your responsibility. With constant communication, the changes both in the relationship and individually can bring excitement and interest all your life.

MONEY AND EMPLOYMENT

Money can be the source of pleasure or a lot of problems. Sex and communication are usually the reason for relationship break-up, but finance can be the catalyst. Whatever your income, there is never enough. Expectations continually rise. Some people pretend they have a lot of money to impress a potential partner, causing a let-down once a relationship is established. Do you use money to give you status or self-worth? Were you both working and independent financially when you met? Possibly parents were generous when you were single. Once in a relationship things can change dramatically. Maybe you have taken on a heavy mortgage, other financial commitments or a large loan. Perhaps children have come along. Arguments over money are common. Are you the careful one and your partner reckless, or the other way round? It is so easy to get into debt. Mail order catalogues, hire purchase agreements, store cards, slot machines, or gambling all absorb money. Unless kept in check, money problems can take years to pay back. Have you agreed on a budget?

Sticking to it is not always easy but if things are worked out jointly, at least there are no terrible surprises. It can be devastating to a relationship when joint money is found to have been frittered away. If there are children from a previous relationship, this can add an extra strain. There may be maintenance to pay, putting a strain on finances. The problem can be made worse if money and presents are used to try to assuage guilt for the hurt caused by a breakup. Jealousy and resentment can result.

Having a baby can bring financial pressures. If you both wish to carry on working, or have to, there is the problem of child minders, baby-sitters or an au pair. Working hard and coping with the needs of a family can be exhausting. There is little time for the relationship and the pressures can take their toll. Maybe you decide that one partner stays at home. The main breadwinner might have to take on extra shifts or work longer hours to make ends meet. Both partners need support but often neither has the energy, understanding or time to devote to each other. Taking time off work to help with children can be a source of disagreement. Illness, school holidays or even the school play can cause difficulties. Using up holiday allowance or giving up pay can add to the stress.

Do you have a job you enjoy? Because of financial pressures you may feel stuck. Maybe it costs too much money to retrain. Commuting to work or unsociable hours may make the problem worse. Do you get support or feel taken for granted by your partner? Perhaps you take your frustrations out on each other or, alternatively, withdraw into yourself. Losing a job or being made redundant can be devastating. You may feel defined by your job, status and income, and without it you feel worthless. Being at home on your own, missing friends at work or the challenges of a job can be difficult. It is a good time to reassess who you are and the direction you wish your life to go. New opportunities will present themselves. Don't keep yourself to yourself. Your loss in income might be caused by illness, making finance really tight. Whatever the situation, it might be worth finding out your rights regarding Social Security.

You may be lucky enough to win money, receive an inheritance or do well at work. It is most people's dream to be wealthy. A lot of money can give you the freedom to do what you want and security for the future. However, letting go of an old lifestyle may not be as easy as you imagined. There may be a different social scene, a new district or new domestic expectations. Your partner may not wish to move or have different ideas of what money is for. You may want to support lots of charities or worthy causes. Perhaps you want to save or, alternatively, spend, spend, spend. Maybe you want the family to benefit. A lot of money, as with too little, can cause relationship problems unless there is good communication.

Have you made an up-to-date will? Living together does not mean your partner necessarily inherits. A new will might have to be made when marrying, on divorce or separation, on the birth of a child or any major change in your financial circumstances such as retirement or buying a home. Tell your family who your executors are and where your will can be found. If you have children, it can cause problems if you have not specified who their guardians should be. Unless you make out a will, it is unlikely that your worldly goods will be distributed in the way that you wanted. Inheritance tax planning may be necessary. Perhaps there are other family members you ought to consider? Once again, communication is important.

If you are getting married, what about a pre-nuptial agreement? It is so easy when you are in love to imagine nothing will ever go wrong. Hopefully it never will. Do you know where all the paper work regarding finance is kept? Have you considered pensions and worked out what you may be entitled to in older age? Widowhood can bring nasty surprises. A joint account may save the problem of access to money in the immediate aftermath of a death. It is so sad if families fall out over inheritance because of lack of financial planning. Now is the time to sort things out if you have not already done so.

Exercise (viii) Priorities in a relationship

Out of this list, which do you think are the most important in a relationship? What order would you put them? Ask your partner to do the same.

Listening
Learning
Loving
Looking
Laughing
Socialising

CHAPTER TEN — BABY BLISS OR BABY BLUES

PREGNANCY

For most couples, having a child is the greatest joy. To make another human being together and watch your child grow can be a wonderful and rewarding experience. Before embarking on this journey, have you asked yourself, do you want children? Do you really both want children? If your relationship was based on not starting a family, it can be difficult if you or your partner start to think differently. Some people do not want children because of a career, bad past experiences or lack of parental feeling. You may be concerned about having a damaged child, passing on a genetic problem or just feel the world is not a safe place for children. Other people's children or younger brothers or sisters may have put you off parenthood. Perhaps you imagine you will not make a good parent, or be unable to cope. Are you worried you may lose your freedom or become boring or less attractive? These are real but often unfounded fears, and talking to other parents or your doctor may put your mind at rest.

Are there more reasons other than starting a family that you hope for pregnancy? Attempting to revive a floundering relationship, or to trap a partner by having a baby is not advisable. Maybe you think having a baby will give you an opportunity to leave home, be rehoused or leave work. You may feel pressure from parents to produce a grandchild or feel left out when friends have children. Getting older or being bored could be your motivation. Are you facing a new life when older children go off to school? Perhaps you feel pressured by society to have a baby before it is too late. A woman's fertility time clock is ticking. Whatever your reason, the reality of having a baby, the long-term implications and responsibility should not be ignored. Some intend to be a one-parent family, many do not, but looking after a baby alone is not easy.

Deciding when to have a baby can depend on many things. Being married or in a very steady relationship is the ideal. Possibly in a gay relationship you are considering parenthood. Have you got a home or are you still with your parents? What about the financial implications? There may be a loss of income making things difficult. Timing can make a difference to your allowances and it is often worth checking this out. If there are other children, the age gap between them may be important. Despite lots of planning, things can go wrong. Maybe the pregnancy happened quicker than you thought. Or, alternatively, conceiving may not be easy.

Are you or your partner having fertility problems? Medical science has advanced so much in this field, and it is worth discussing any problems with your doctor. There may be a simple answer to your difficulties. Alternatively, you may have to face some form of treatment. It is not always easy and in some cases very expensive. For some types of problem, you may have to have sex at particular times of heightened fertility. This can be stressful, and sex can become a chore. A lot of understanding and support is needed as you face each monthly period. Setbacks are upsetting, and relationships can become tense. Unfortunately, for some, there is no hope of pregnancy. There is often a bereavement reaction, and it can take some time to come to terms with the situation. Adoption could be considered, but it is not for everyone.

Pregnancy may happen by mistake. Maybe you already have your family and do not want any more children. Contraception can fail sometimes. Perhaps pregnancy is a result of a drunken fling, a holiday romance, sexual abuse or rape. Sexual experimentation may have got out of hand or your understanding of the facts of life may be limited. You may have imagined that a woman near the menopause or having just given birth is safe. Unplanned or unintentional pregnancies can be greeted with great happiness, but

114

for some the implications are very difficult. The circumstances may cause great social, medical or financial problems. Perhaps you consider you are too young or too old. Now what? If you do not want the baby, any decision should not be taken lightly. Speak to your doctor or a counsellor and get as much help and information as possible. Parents, close friends or partners will have a point of view, but in the end what you do is your decision. It is your baby and you will have to live with any decision you make for years to come. You may choose to have the baby adopted. Alternatively, an abortion may be offered. Whether you make the decision as a partnership or alone, think hard about what you are doing. For some, an abortion is a medical necessity. There may be complications, a test showing abnormalities or the baby may have died in the womb. You should be offered counselling for any abortion. For some, the reaction afterwards is difficult and not always anticipated.

Once pregnant, some women positively bloom. Others have to face months of illness, hospital visits and discomfort. There may be early morning sickness, irritability or tiredness. It is a time to stop smoking and eat the right food. It is not always easy for a woman to feel sexy during this time, and both partners need to discuss feelings. You may be concerned that sexual activity might somehow damage the baby. Unless advised by the doctor, there is no reason why normal sexual activity cannot continue, if you both agree. Some men begin to feel jealous as the centre of attention shifts to the mother and baby. Remember the relationship needs nurturing too. The original euphoria of the pregnancy can wear off during the nine-month wait.

Where possible, both partners should be included in all the preparations. Attending classes is a wonderful way to meet other mums and dads and share feelings and concerns. Are you going to be together at the birth? What about paternity and maternity leave? Have you chosen the names? Do you agree? Hospital stay after the birth of a baby is quite short, unless there are complications. Who is going to be at home when the baby is brought home from hospital? Perhaps a home birth is possible. What about baby clothes, prams, and other equipment? Are you going to get second-hand from relatives or friends or buy new? If there is another child or children at home, why not consider giving a present from the new baby to make them feel special too.

For some people, pregnancy does not go smoothly. There may be complications and sometimes a loss. A miscarriage affects people in different ways. It may feel like the end of the world for some while others take it in their stride. You may console yourself that it was meant by God, or the child may have been born damaged or deformed. There may never be an explanation. The loss of a baby before it is even born can be devastating. You may wonder if you will ever get over the loss. The resulting bereavement is not always understood by both partners and can cause difficulties. A stillbirth can be even more upsetting. You may be able to see and hold the baby. There will probably be a funeral to go through. Returning to everyday life and answering the question 'What did you have?' is not easy.

THE BIRTH

The first sign something is happening may be the waters breaking. For some it is the contractions. In the case of possible problems or assisted birth, a date to attend hospital may be advised. Giving birth is an experience that affects people in different ways. Contractions may go on for some time, while others hardly feel a thing. The birth itself can be a very happy occasion. Babies do not always come on time. Your baby might arrive prematurely or be helped to arrive early because of complications. It can be worrying but everything will be done to help. Some babies do not seem to want to be born and may have to be induced. On occasions a caesarean is suggested if natural birth proves difficult. Doctors and nurses will do all they can to reassure and advise you. Giving birth for some is quite spiritual. Others find it frightening and a shock. Watching the birth can be a life-changing experience. After the birth there may be medical intervention of some sort. Stitches are quite common. No one can predict how you might feel. Everything will be done to help you and your baby.

Once presented with a baby, the joy can be overwhelming. It seems like a miracle that you have made a baby. Not all births are greeted with euphoria though, and you may not feel as you imagined. Not everyone bonds or feels close to the baby straight away. Never feel a failure. There may be tears or the baby blues after a day or so. Unexpected feelings of loss or even resentment might occur. Perhaps you hoped for a baby of a particular sex. You may be confronted with a multiple birth and are struggling with the implications. Finance, family interference, relationship problems or general health may have an influence on how you feel. Ask for help if you are at all worried about your reaction. Is the baby going to be breastfed or not? Not all mums want to and some are unable to breastfeed. A lot of advice and support is available.

Post-natal depression is difficult to understand. After looking forward to the baby, a new mum might find she is not so sure it was such a good idea. Feelings of loss prevail. The emotions can be overwhelming. If you think about the changes in a woman's life when having a baby, it is not surprising that there is some reaction. She has changed, lost some of her freedom, possibly left her job and missing contact with work or friends. Her figure might have altered. Perhaps she has put on a lot of weight or lost it. She may no longer feel young and sexy. Bonding might be difficult, and she might feel a sense of failure. The relationship with her partner is no longer exclusive. There is another in his life. She has lost the person she used to be. Her time is taken up with the baby, and it is exhausting. It is easy to imagine that all other women cope. Perhaps there are expectations on how a new mum ought to feel or behave and possibly family pressure to do things in certain ways. Being diagnosed with post-natal depression does not mean a woman is mentally deranged or that she will continually feel depressed. There is a lot of help available, and the problem is well understood. Get help rather than struggle on. Being a new mum is difficult enough without feeling depressed. Never leave things to the point when either mother or baby is in danger.

Some babies sleep well and are easy, while others are not. It is no reflection on the parents. Sleepless nights, continual crying and never-ending washing can stretch patience to breaking point. Both partners can get exhausted, especially if you are trying to hold down jobs as well. It is so easy to start bickering at each other. A partner can resent the fact that meals do not happen on time or housework is not done. Both partners might feel misunderstood. Maybe there is not enough help. A partner might need reminding it is their baby too. Accepting these feelings and talking about the problems helps. Sharing the joys and the difficulties of parenthood can cement a relationship. Watching the changes in your baby, delighting in its funny ways and enjoying the fact that you are now a family is extremely rewarding. Some like to celebrate the birth of their child. Does your religion or belief have some sort of ceremony, perhaps a naming or thanksgiving service? Are you going to have your child baptised?

You may have to face the tragic fact that your child is disabled or retarded. There is no answer to your pain. There may be blame, guilt or feelings of terrible disappointment, none of which make coping easy. Some find it easy to love a child no matter what situation, while others struggle with guilt and non-acceptance. Get as much help and advice as you can. Accept the tears and help each other to express emotion and feelings. There are other parents who have gone through similar suffering, and there are organisations who understand if you ask.

Having a baby opens up a whole new world. You join the ranks of millions of others who have shared your experience in some way. Complete strangers will stop you in the street to admire the baby or commiserate if you are facing problems. You are responsible for someone who relies on you totally. You may feel needed, sometimes overwhelmed, but special. The miracle of birth and creating a new human being can be the most wonderful and rewarding experience. You may spend hours just watching as you marvel at the new creation. Enjoy your baby.

CHAPTER ELEVEN — THE UPS AND DOWNS OF FAMILY LIFE

Each stage of a child's life has its pleasures and its problems. Perhaps you have had some experience in caring for other people's babies or have younger brothers or sisters. Parenting means different things to different people. You may be bringing up a child as a couple or coping on your own. Are you both working or is one partner staying at home while the other goes out to work? For some, being at home is very lonely. Domesticity and the demands of a young child are not for them. Maybe you both have to work for financial reasons. It can be a difficult time as tiredness and stress can take its toll.

One partner does not always understand the pressures suffered by the other, and the relationship can be strained as a result. A young child is very demanding, and being a parent is often harder than imagined. There is no shame in asking for help. Your child may have difficulties sleeping or feeding. Maybe tantrums are a problem. The physical pressures of not getting enough sleep, extra financial commitments or expectations can take their toll. A childminder or nanny can be wonderful, if you can afford it, but there are many tales of problems too. Make sure you check the credentials. You may be lucky enough to have parents who are happy to help with childminding. You could share the care with a friend who also has children.

As with any new experience in life, there are often unforeseen emotional problems. A parent or a partner might be critical of your methods of bringing up your child. Parents may be interfering, or in some cases try to take over. You may lack confidence in your own ability. There will be times when you feel at your wit's end. Do you talk to other parents? You will find most feel just the same. Joining a mums and toddler group may help overcome the isolation and loneliness felt by many. It is no reflection on your ability to be a good parent.

Is the child you are looking after your own? It may be adopted, fostered or from your partner's previous relationship. The anxiety to show you are a good parent may add extra strain. Despite your love for your partner, you may not have appreciated the extent of your role as a parent. Do you battle to be accepted as a step-mum or dad? Perhaps there was a tragedy or family break-up and the responsibilities of parenthood were thrust upon you. There are so many different parental roles. Are you only a part-timer, sharing the responsibilities of your child with your ex- partner? Maybe parenting is just a weekend experience for you. A court order may give only limited access, causing a lot of stress and heart ache.

Having a large family has its rewards. Every child brings its own individual personality and pleasure. Trying to be fair all the time is not easy. Showing any favouritism can cause upsets both in your partnership and the relationship between children. Do you agree about the discipline and how to administer punishment? It can be the cause of disagreements. What is suitable for one child may not have the same response from another. There may be sibling rivalry or jealousies. One child may be better looking, more intelligent or have a more engaging personality than another. Showing you care for each child the same can be difficult at times. Emphasising their individual qualities does help their confidence.

If you take on step-children, other factors have to be taken into account. One parent might want to compensate for any hurt caused by a break-up, while the other children resent any favours. The ex-partner may cause difficulties regarding access and parental responsibilities. Do you use the child as a pawn in an unresolved bitter dispute over money and rights? There may be court cases, reports by social workers, difficulties with ex-grand-parents, or problems with the separation of siblings. A child may be troubled and upset at leaving one parent. A lot of talking is helpful. Bring things out into the open, and discuss things amicably if you can. Remember it is not the child's fault.

TODDLERS

Having a toddler around the house is exhausting. The house has to change. Things have to be moved higher, cupboards locked and gates put up. The speed children move is amazing. They follow you everywhere. 'The terrible twos' is a difficult experience for many people. Toddlers look so angelic and do wonderful things but can be exasperating. Tempers can get very short. You may find you are not as placid as you imagined. Frustration and tiredness can be difficult. If you feel in danger of damaging your child, get help. All your theories about childcare will be tested to the limit. It always seems your child is the only one still in nappies, having tantrums or behaving badly. Everyone feels a failure at times, but no one is asking for perfection. Love is what your child needs. Your partner's upbringing and attitudes may be very different to your own. Put time aside to talk together about your feelings or any difficulties you may have.

Do you try and get baby-sitters occasionally and get out together? You are not just parents, but sexual, fun-loving people too. Arrange family outings, visits and walks if you can. Mum and toddler groups provide a place where you can share the joys of parenthood or have a moan. Sometimes care is available to look after the toddlers during a talk or demonstration. Nursery schools, play groups or crèches are all available too. There is considerable debate as to what is best for a child to give it a good start in life. Do childminders give your child enough stimulation? Does a child gain social skills by being in a nursery school? Do you start to teach reading yourself? These and many other factors are worth considering, but fashions and theories continually change. You have to do what you consider right for your child. Different children mature at different rates so comparisons are not necessarily helpful. There are courses available now for parenting skills. If you, and possibly your partner, are having problems, a course will help to give you more confidence and some good coping strategies.

SCHOOL DAYS

School days can bring new challenges. Is your local school suitable? There may be costs involved, uniforms to buy, or even a move to a new area to qualify for a particular school. The first day at school may be just as hard for you as it is for your child. It is the end of an era. You are handing over control of your child to someone else. For some parents, the grief reaction is quite unexpected. It may be made more difficult if your child does not settle. For a non-working partner, there is a big gap in life once a child starts school. There is time for you, but it is difficult to know how to fill it at first. Taking and fetching times can cut into your day. There are school holidays, 'in service' days or times of sickness to consider. Is your partner or anyone else able to help should you return to work? Friends sometimes share transport. This is also when grandparents can be invaluable. There are sports days, open days, plays and concerts to attend. To add to the pressure, after-school activities require transportation. Just at the time you would like to relax in the evening, your child may be tired and irritable.

The influence of other people's children is not always positive. Manners, language and general behaviour can deteriorate. Meeting other parents outside school or at school functions can help you to realise you are not alone. How much television do you allow? Who listens to the reading or tests the spellings? Juggling a job, children and the home can be a terrific strain, and it is a time when a relationship can get neglected. Check to see if your partner is happy, and talk about your feelings. Rows in front of a child will cause insecurity, and the child's behaviour will reflect these feelings. Violence, alcohol-fuelled behaviour by parents or continual bickering does not give a good role model. Think hard about what effect it is having. As an exercise, imagine if your child was suddenly orphaned. How would they remember you?

TEENAGERS

There is often a struggle as your child tries his or her wings in an attempt to be independent. Your influence becomes less and less, and yet you are still needed. How much to let go is very difficult and can cause tensions. Boyfriends and girlfriends, who come on the scene, might not be your choice. Music seems too loud, the bedroom a tip and home treated like a hotel. Fashion may seem outrageous. It is a time of lots of homework, revision, projects and exams, all creating stress. Try to remember your teenage years and your feelings.

The modern-day influences project children into an adult world often long before they are ready. They are bombarded with fashion demands, explicit sex, violence or emotional drama, difficult enough to cope with at any age. At the same time, they are developing physically, having unexpected and new feelings and trying to find themselves. School life puts pressure on too. They are required to choose subjects, a career or college, often with little understanding of what they really want. Drugs and alcohol, unwanted pregnancy, AIDS and other diseases all add to the worry for parents trying to help steer their children through life. Keep talking and recognise the difficulties. If they should go off the rails, get as much help as you can.

When a child really does cause problems, it is easy to blame yourself or your partner, neither of which may be true. Try and analyse the reasons why your child is reacting. Are there too many pressures, bullying at school or a feeling of failure? Emotional outbursts are often a way to cover up hurt inside. Show as much love as you can and try to get them to talk. School counsellors can help if there is a problem at school. Talking things through with an outsider can be easier sometimes. Drug addiction can be a terrible problem. It can happen in any family. Has your child got into the wrong crowd? For some, their metabolism reacts badly to drugs and experimentation leads to addiction. Get as much help as you can for both you and your child. In the end, an addict has to recognise his or her problem and change. You cannot do it for them.

You may have to face other problems with your child. A disease, illness or accident may have affected their looks, mobility or behaviour in a permanent way. There may be a mental illness or deep depression. Wild swings of emotion, violence or abuse is not easy to accept. They may be incapable of looking after themselves physically or mentally. Ask for help. It might be difficult to accept your child has changed and perhaps will never be as you hoped. Although different, they still need love and understanding. It can feel like bereavement as you come to terms with the loss of expectations. Your life may be turned upside down by new demands of illness or disability.

When eventually a child leaves home, it can be a great relief. Others suffer the grief of the empty nest syndrome. Your reaction may be quite unexpected. You have devoted your life to your child, done all the things you were supposed to do, now what? You have your life to lead and for the first time the freedom to do things for yourself. It is easy to hide behind children and never look at yourself as a person in your own right. What now?

CHAPTER TWELVE — CRISES IN RELATIONSHIPS

AN AFFAIR

Finding out your partner is having an affair is devastating. Perhaps it is a one-night stand or you may have had your suspicions for some time. Was the discovery accidental or the information given by someone else? Maybe you were the last to know. Your partner might make a confession or just leaves with no explanation. Who is it with? Your best friend, a work colleague, a member of your family, someone you trusted or a complete stranger? The shock can be overwhelming. Grief sets in. The trust in the partner you thought you knew has gone. There will be questions about sexually transmitted diseases, AIDS or pregnancy. What about the contraception? Your relationship is no longer how you imagined. Your friends and family may be affected, and life changes dramatically. There is often anger, tears, disbelief and recrimination. Accusations start to fly. Sometimes there is a feeling of inadequacy, numbness or disbelief. You might be tempted to hurt back. When feelings are high, it is not the time to make decisions that can be regretted later.

It may be you having an affair. The 'spark, spark' feeling of a new relationship can be intoxicating. The sense of danger and the fact that the relationship is not allowed adds an extra edge. It is so easy to think it is love. Perhaps your affair has introduced you to a better sex life. You may imagine you can keep two relationships. Not easy, as you can so easily be found out. Unfortunately, there are not many people who are prepared to forgive a partner's affair. Perhaps you really do want to get out of your relationship. Maybe you are genuinely in love. Think hard about the consequences. Is your new partner married already? He, or she, may be a serial philanderer. Would you be able to trust if you were married? Do not underestimate their present partner if they find out. A future together might be fraught or impossible.

There are many and varied reasons why people have an affair. Here are some reasons offered:

The relationship was stale
I was seduced
I was lonely while away from home
He/she seemed to really understand me
Sex had gone off in our relationship
I needed to recapture youth
I only married to get away from home
We used to be lovers
Revenge

My partner didn't keep up socially
I realise I am homosexual
I was drunk, it didn't mean anything
I was seeking sexual reassurance
We shared the same interests
I was offered comfort in a time of trouble
I have a high sex drive
I always fancied him/her
I fell out of love
I wanted to find out what it is like with someone else
I felt more loved and wanted
He/she was more attractive/younger/richer
I married too young
My partner seemed like a brother/sister

Some are a cry for help. Maybe the relationship has been allowed to go stale or sex has got less exciting or ceased. Communication may have broken down as each attends to their own interests or jobs. Children may have been the centre of attention and no time given to the relationship. There are usually two sides to every problem — a concept not easy to accept at first. An affair need not be the end of a relationship. If your partner does not know, the guilt can be difficult. Do you tell or not? Help can be found if needed. For some, an affair brings a new understanding. A richer and better relationship can develop with new understandings of each other's needs. Trust can return. It may not be easy to accept a partner back or go back to a relationship, but many a couple regret taking an instant decision to divorce or separate. "If only we had tried harder" is often the cry, but unfortunately for some there is no other option but to break up.

ABUSE

Abuse can take many forms. You may be constantly belittled, told you are useless or humiliated in front of family or friends. There may be bullying, threats, hitting, physical or sexual assault, or even rape. Violent assault is a criminal offence, and help is available from the police. There are a lot of agencies that can give you advice and support should you need it, whether you are the perpetrator or the victim. Abuse, more often than not is against women, but it can be the other way round. Why does a relationship turn abusive? Were there signs of aggression before marriage? Often possessiveness or control is considered flattering while courting and any violence is forgiven. Sometimes there is pattern of abuse in a family. Parents may have been violent to each other or towards the children. Brothers or sisters might have been controlling and abusive. They could become role models for the future.

Abuse is to do with power or control. Individuals who abuse may have been damaged in past relationships, belittled by parents, experienced aggressive discipline or degraded sexually. In some cases a homosexual experience or unwanted sex in childhood may cause a feeling of shame or muddled emotion. These deep inner painful feelings are kept hidden. The vulnerability is covered up by over dominant behaviour and aggression to avoid being found out or hurt again. There is an inner fear and often a lack of confidence in sexuality. Controlling others or their surroundings by violence or threats covers the fears.

Individuals with an inner vulnerability sometimes choose emotionally strong, caring partners. Their partners may themselves have experienced abuse in some form, but perhaps had some help or gained some understanding. Were you like this when you first met? Alternatively, some abusers choose very young or inexperienced partners, thinking they can be moulded and see them as a possession and someone to do their will. Abusers are often charming, very attentive and loving at the beginning. They may put you up on a pedestal and treat you like some sort of god or goddess. There may be some sob story about their past, giving only one side of what really happened. Perhaps an ex-partner treated them badly, they were wronged or misunderstood. Is drink or drugs an issue? Did you feel you could 'save' them? At the beginning the devotion to each other is often exclusive. Friends are dropped, and even family can be blocked out. Does this all sound familiar?

The problem can start if you try to be more independent. Perhaps you get a new job or a new friend. Even a new outfit or underwear can start accusations. Lingering at the shops or spending any time away from home can seem a threat to the relationship. A baby may be taking up your time and energy and problems may arise as attention shifts to a child. Your partner is no longer the total centre of your life. Accusations start to fly as the inner fear of being belittled or out of control sets in. Abuse can start. In this situation you may be accused of affairs or degraded in social situations. Your looks criticised and your housework or parenting skills questioned. The insecure partner will insist they are always right, and you start to lose confidence. They hate to feel they are the underdog and will try to convince you that other people are wrong, interfering and bad. Your parents, your friends, the doctor, other drivers, in fact, everyone will be seen as a threat. They might attempt to control everything you think or do. Sex may be used as a weapon. An abuser may have affairs to punish you, or say or do things to degrade your sex. Do you imagine it is your fault? Many feel the punishment is justified at first because they are told they are responsible, but can soon be dominated by fear.

After an outburst, there is often a making-up time when you may revert to the original devotion, but the abuse happens again. Injuries might be covered up or denied. You may still be in love and not wishing to upset the family or lose the relationship. If the situation gets bad, you may seek another relationship to get reassurance, making matters much worse. Thoughts of leaving may be met with dire threats against you or the children. If you get away, you are pursued. There may be threats of violence or suicide unless you return. Are you in this situation? Get help and legal advice before you do anything. Your actions could affect the rights to the house or children. If children are involved in any violence, something must be done. It is not failure to seek help.

It is often asked why some people stay in an abusive relationship. It can take a long time for someone to realise they can get out or that they have a right to be themselves. They begin to believe they are worthless and that they are lucky to have any partner at all. Some stay because the making up after abuse is most enjoyable and intense. The relationship reverts back to how it was at the beginning for a while. Others learn how to control an abusive relationship by working out ways to cope. Praise might be used to make their partner feel better, or a submissive role might be taken occasionally to restore the balance of power. Some see their partner as strong and feel protected. Every situation is different, and the appropriate action for each relationship should be sought. As relationships mature and with new understandings, things can improve in some cases.

Recognising each other's role in the relationship problem is important. Without this recognition, the situation can be repeated in future relationships. You may go on, with your caring ways, to choose another lame duck.

BREAKING UP AND DIVORCE

As the saying goes' Breaking up is hard to do'. Whether you are the one who wants out, or your partner, someone usually gets hurt. Divorce has to be seen as the last resort. The problems may have been there for some time and the situation intolerable. You may not be speaking at all. There may be threats or violence. Bitterness, resentment, anger and hate sour the situation even further. Children might be involved in a custody battle, and the emotional damage caused can be devastating. On the other hand, you may be in a relationship where you mutually agree to part and things are amicable. Maybe it is you who want to leave and you have to cope with a pleading partner, or in some cases even threatened suicide. There may be feelings of guilt, worry over family reaction or fear of social isolation. Even questions of who will have the family pet can cause deep emotions.

If handled well, everyone concerned can eventually move on in life. For some, the pain consumes their character and affects all future relationships. Children may be damaged if their feelings are ignored, being pulled in all directions as parents fight it out. Ask for help. There are so many issues to be resolved. The children, the home, furniture, finance, pension rights and possibly other things you have not thought of. Before leaving home or taking any irrevocable action, seek legal advice. A visit to a Citizen's Advice Bureau is extremely useful if you are not sure what to do. There are conciliation services available to help you sort things out. Agreeing amicably on the eventual outcome can save a lot of heartache.

If children are involved, trying to explain is difficult. It is important to emphasise a divorce is not their fault. It is not necessarily helpful to tell a child the reason for the breakdown is 'falling out of love'. It implies there is no fault. Be prepared to admit mistakes and failings on both sides. A continual barrage of abuse regarding the ex-partner will not help the child. They are half of them after all. In some cases, children are denied access to a parent by law. Where possible, each parent should continue to give love so that children can grow in the knowledge of their worth. You may find that even if you wanted to break-up, you have a grief reaction. A relationship has died. You may look back at the happy times you had with great sadness. Children feel this too and can often act it out by doing badly at school or becoming withdrawn. Aggression or abuse may be used by others to cover up their inner pain. Talking through feelings helps considerably, when they are ready to do so.

CHAPTER THIRTEEN —
BEREAVEMENT

The subject of death is difficult for a lot of people to talk about. When was your first experience of death? For many, it may be the loss of a family pet, an important part of the family. A national disaster or death of a prominent personality might have provoked deep feelings. You may have read about terrible deaths in wars, been upset at losses depicted on films or be moved by others' tragedies. It is the death of one of your close relatives, friends or loved ones when true bereavement becomes reality. Illnesses, accidents and tragedies happen any age, any time. No one knows exactly how they will feel until faced with a situation of loss. You may imagine what you will do or be convinced of your reaction, but emotions and behaviour are often quite different.

FACING DEATH AS A CHILD

Children can find it hard to cope with death. Have you had to face the loss of a parent, close grandparent, brother, sister or friend when young? Maybe your life had to change dramatically as a result. Losing your support system at a young age can take away your childhood. Were your feelings taken into account? Perhaps you were not allowed to attend the funeral or kept out of the way. You may have been swamped with kindness, in the hope you will be shielded from the pain of loss. The subject of death may never have been discussed at the time or since. What did you do with your emotions as a result? Has anyone ever listened to your inner thoughts?

For some, death causes little or no reaction at the time. Grief can come out years later. Inwardly, you may grieve about lost innocence, lost closeness or lost love, not realising why. Are you suffering from the impact now? At the time of a death, you may have been busy at school, facing exams or looking after younger siblings. You may have stifled your feelings not to upset others. Perhaps it is only now you are suffering with feelings of inner emptiness. Bereavement may have been expressed by you in different ways in the past. Did you rebel, become disruptive or retreat into a shell? Concentration on school work is often difficult, especially if emotion is misunderstood by others.

There can be positives from bereavement. Despite the tragedy, the insights gained can help your maturity. Your experience and emotional understanding may help you to understand others facing loss. You will discover new strengths you never thought you had, as your life has to change. Some people may become close while others drift away, giving you the opportunity to make new friends.

INITIAL EMOTIONS

The first real loss in your life has a big impact. The expectation that everyone experiences grief the same is unreal. There is no right or wrong way to grieve. It depends a lot on your personality, the depth of the relationship or the circumstances of death. Whether you are an emotional mess or believe in a stiff upper lip, it is no reflection on how much you care. The death may have been sudden, an accident, a fatal heart attack or unexpected illness. In some cases, there is no time to say goodbye or talk about feelings. Even a predicted loss is a shock. You always hope for a miracle. It is so hard to believe it is the end of someone's life. You may feel they will walk in the room any minute, return from a holiday or still be in that bed or chair.

Feelings sometimes are unexpected or misunderstood. After a long illness, there can be a sense of freedom, a release both for you and for them. There may not be any grief initially at all. You might feel they are in a better place, away from pain or relieved from a life not worth living. In cases of really old age, there may not be much sadness but a celebration of a life well lived. Sadly for some, there is the heart-breaking decision of switching off a life support machine. Feelings of guilt are not unusual despite reassurance that nothing can be done. Guilt may add to your distress in other ways too. Watching helplessly, unable or unskilled to prevent a death is not easy. It may spur you on to do a first aid course or join a charity to help the cause. Some go over and over in their mind how it could have been so different. Anger may be another unexpected emotion. Hospitals, doctors, other relatives or God may be blamed. There may be a great desire to take revenge in some way or hit out at society. Being physically violent to relieve tension or anger can cause more problems. It does not take the pain of loss away.

For many, bereavement opens the floodgates of emotion. The tears just will not stop. Sleep is often difficult, and you may feel you are going mad. Life seems pointless. There is a terrible emptiness, an inner pain, as if something has been taken from your body. The loss may cause you to have to change your lifestyle. Do you have to move; is there a money problem or family fallout? If you have been the carer, your days will feel very empty. Who wants you or needs you now? Finding things to do to fill your days takes time. Life will seem without purpose for a while. Perhaps you have lost someone you confided in, or saw on a very regular basis. There is so often a double loss as your old life style dies too.

Suicidal feelings can be very real at this time. Self-harm will not bring the person back. You may feel you want to be with them or cannot cope without them. Ask yourself these questions first. Are you sure you will go to the same place if you did die? Will they be pleased to see you or more upset you have taken your life? Will they feel all their input in your life was worthwhile? Is there life after death? How will others cope if they are faced with your death too? How would you want to be remembered? Who would come to your funeral?

The following imagery might help you to understand your importance in life after you have lost someone. Death is like a pebble falling in a pond. The relatives, friends and loved ones are the ripples who carry the memory on of a loved one. The affection, funny ways, sayings and special things they did will never die while you are alive and the world might be a better place as a result. You are extremely important to give meaning to their life. Emotions after a death can be very hard to understand, but things will eventually get easier. If you are really struggling, ask for help from your doctor. He or she will be able to advise you and possibly give you medication to get over a difficult time. Do not struggle alone.

Being with someone who is dying can be different in every case. It may be terribly sad, or a great privilege or a terrifying experience. Some people drift away in their sleep, serene and at peace as they face their last breath. At the point of death, doctors do all they can to make the stress of passing easier. Watching someone in pain, fear or emotion may make parting difficult and have a big impact on your grief. Being at an accident or having to see and experience shocking events, adds to your distress. The last image of someone dying can remain with you for a while. Flashbacks or nightmares can make sleeping difficult. Eventually, happy memories of past times will return, but you can never bring back your loss of innocence. There is a lot more understanding now of shock and the impact it can have, so get support should you feel you need help. The chapter on mental illness may help.

A death may be of someone who is a pivotal family member. The whole family may fall apart as a result. Without a parent or grandparent, a support system may disappear. Alternatively, a loss might bring the family together for the first time. Does the family turn to you for comfort? Maybe you take it on yourself to help others with their grief. Your own grief will be put on hold. Have you lost a close friend? Friends are so important and a huge gap will be left in your life. The death of a baby or young child is particularly tragic. Parents expect to go first, and the pain of loss never goes completely. The death of a brother or sister can change the dynamics in a family. Pressure can be put on to another child to fill the role or, alternatively, always be compared. Remembrance is important, but making out anyone who dies is a saint is not necessarily helpful. See them as they really were, warts and all, and love them for what they meant to you in life.

A stillbirth, miscarriage or necessary abortion can have devastating results, not always understood. Although you never had the chance to get to know your child, they were real to you. There was a baby and it died. You may always wonder what it would have been like. Others may not realize how you grieve. Maybe you chose to have an abortion, an intentional loss of a baby. The reasons why are not always appreciated by outsiders. At first, there may be great relief, but years later the impact of the loss can cause great grief, often experienced alone.

Losing a partner can be especially difficult. Having shared your inner secrets, enjoyed each other's company, laughed, cried and loved together, there is a huge void. No one understands you quite so well. Who is there to remember old friends, share memories or understand your family jokes? You may miss the cuddles and sex. Life will seem empty and meaningless for a while. Some imagine their partner walking in the room, hear their call or even smell them. You may talk to photos or cuddle their clothing in an attempt to reach them. Coping alone with chores, finances or family problems is not easy. Do you feel angry that they have gone away and left you to cope? Paper work, cooking, car maintenance or the ironing may always have been done for you. Facing life alone is not easy, and perhaps more difficult if you have no friends or hobbies. Boredom and aloneness can be a big problem.

The death of someone through suicide is hard to accept. Everyone feels guilty and wonders how they might have helped. Reasons for suicide are not easy to understand. Unable to face a loss of some sort is usually the cause, but deep depression or worthlessness can be the trigger. You may wonder how you could have changed things if they had shared their inner feelings. Why you were not loved enough for them to stay. Suicidal people are so preoccupied with their thoughts. They may feel they were justified in what they did. The consequences are not thought through, leaving partners, parents, family or friends devastated.

THE FUNERAL

Undertakers do a great deal to help with a funeral and do all they can to accommodate the way you want to say goodbye. There may be religious rites to be observed or traditions to be followed. Is there an inquest? Perhaps an autopsy has to be performed. Do you have to identify the body? It can all be stressful and upsetting. The funeral may have to be delayed for weeks. Do you go to the chapel of rest or not? This is your choice and no one should make you. It does not help everyone to see a loved one in death, and you may have other memories you want to keep. What about the funeral arrangements? Is there going to be a thanksgiving service as well? Were there specific requests? Is there to be a cremation or burial? What about the hymns? Who has to be informed? Are there flowers to be ordered or service cards to get printed? What will you wear? There is so much to think about. There will be certificates and paper work to be completed. Funeral directors are usually a great help, and there is a lot of information available.

How will you cope with a funeral? Emotions may be overwhelming or you may be unexpectedly calm and in control. No one should judge feelings on outward appearance. You can cry. It is an opportunity to say good-bye, but it is by no means the end of grief. In some cases, there is no body to grieve over, depriving the bereaved of closure. A death may cause you to reject your faith or alternatively, you may find great comfort in your belief.

OTHER PEOPLE'S REACTION

What others do or say after bereavement can be comforting, helpful and sometimes quite overwhelming. You may get unexpected kindness by people you hardly know. On the other hand, some friends and relations may not be there to help. It does not necessarily mean they do not care. Some find loss very difficult to face. They do not know what to say. Fear of emotion or causing emotion holds people back. Some might avoid you, cross to the other side of the street or seem unfriendly. They may say inappropriate things or just stare. Do not condemn too quickly. If they have never had a loss in their own lives, they may not understand the depth of despair you feel. Learn from them what to do or not to do. One day you may be in a situation to comfort others, and your experience will help you understand their feelings.

A death can sometimes cause family feuds. There may be disagreements about the funeral and how it is arranged. Perhaps there are difficulties if certain people attend. Who pays for what? The cost of the funeral, the cars and the grave stone or plaque can be a cause of controversy. Is there agreement about flowers or money to a charity? The inscription and how it is worded or the announcement in the paper all have a potential for family dispute. When it comes to the sharing of possessions, particularly money, things can get nasty. The availability of a will does not necessarily solve the problems. It is so sad when families fall out after a death. Alternatively, if everyone has not met for a long time, there may be an opportunity to clear up some misunderstandings or have a grand reunion.

COPING WITH LOSS

Bereavement goes on and on. It lasts a great deal longer than people imagine. You may cope well and surprise yourself. You may be held up by your belief or the support of family or friends. For some, it is years before they come to terms with a loss. Time does not heal, but you learn to cope better. The feelings of loss can be overwhelming when you least expect. Tears may be difficult to control. A tune, a smell or just a sudden memory can trigger off emotion. You may find you are extremely tired. Getting up in the morning may not be easy. Concentration goes too. Sitting in front of the television, you may not take in anything you see or hear. Reading a book or doing paper work is difficult, and it is hard to relax or feel at peace. Keeping busy sometimes helps. Why not tidy cupboards, empty out drawers or clear the attic? Going out socially can be difficult at first. You often feel lonelier in a crowd. Unfortunately, some people turn to drink to try and drown the pain. This can cause even more problems. Eating for comfort may be another difficulty, while others find their appetite disappearing and reject food. There may be physical reactions to grief. Nervous rashes, headaches, palpitations or panic attacks can result from the stress of bereavement. If suffering from a panic attack, you feel you might die, and it is hard to breathe. Your medical centre or doctor will be able to help you with coping strategies. Sorting out the clothes of a loved one can be stressful. Getting rid of reminders is seen as letting go. As a result, bedrooms are made into shrines, or cupboards never opened. Clearing out is a necessary process on the way to recovery, but should be done when you are ready. Keeping some pictures, perhaps a favourite item or memento is understandable. Some like to plant a tree, buy a piece of furniture or jewellery in memory. What do you intend to do with the ashes, if there are any? Perhaps the family members have views on the subject.

Talking about your loved one is important. Remember them as they were, not as an angel or saint. Each anniversary or birthday brings back painful memories. Visiting a grave or the place where the ashes are scattered is comforting to some. Others may not feel the person is there and choose to remember in their own way. What does death mean? Where are they now? What happens when someone dies? These are all questions you have to answer for yourself. Some turn to faith at this time. You may question the meaning of life and wonder about your own death. You may imagine you have the same illness, will have to face the same fate or will die young. These feelings are quite normal as you struggle with new understandings.

After a death, you may feel your loved one is with you. You may find yourself talking to them. Don't worry, you are not going mad. It is comforting for some to imagine their loved one in a breast pocket and carry them around. Alternatively, you may feel your loved one is far away. Are they in heaven or in some better place? No one knows what happens after death, but we will all be in the same situation one day. Maybe we will all meet again. A death may inspire you to help others, do charity work or fight for human rights. Despite losing someone you love, you gain a lot of new insights and become a more experienced and wiser person. Life is like a tapestry. We live it at the back with all the knots, frayed threads and loose ends. There may be glimpses of the pattern through the maze of tangled thread, but it is not until we reach the other side that the true picture is revealed. It is then and only then that we will understand WHY!